BIG-NOTE PIANO

Disney
Giant Movie Hits

ISBN 0-634-04513-X

Walt Disney Music Company
Wonderland Music Company, Inc.

DISTRIBUTED BY

HAL•LEONARD®
CORPORATION

7777 W. BLUEMOUND RD. P.O. BOX 13819 MILWAUKEE, WI 53213

Visit Hal Leonard Online at
www.halleonard.com

Disney Giant Movie Hits

ARABIAN NIGHTS
from Walt Disney's Aladdin

Lyrics by HOWARD ASHMAN
Music by ALAN MENKEN

Moderately bright

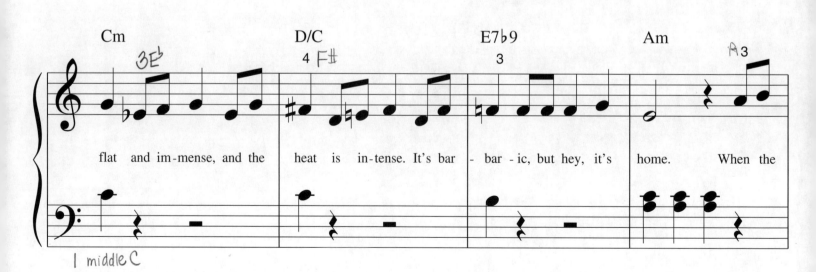

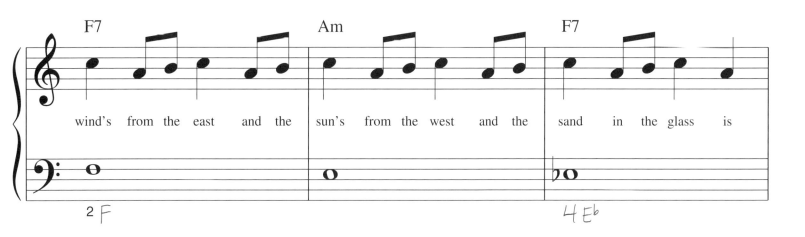

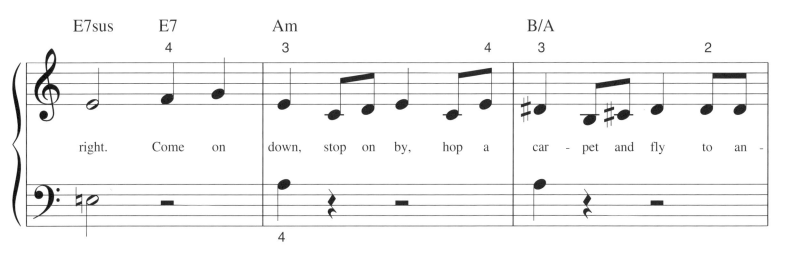

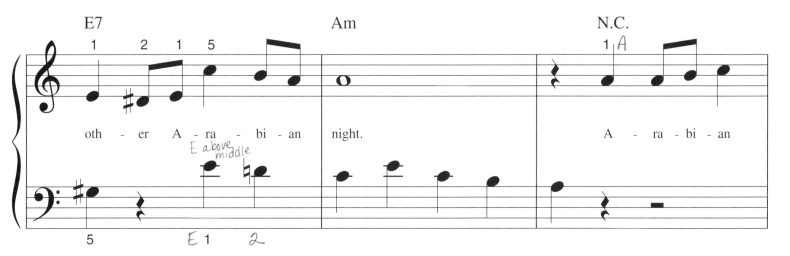

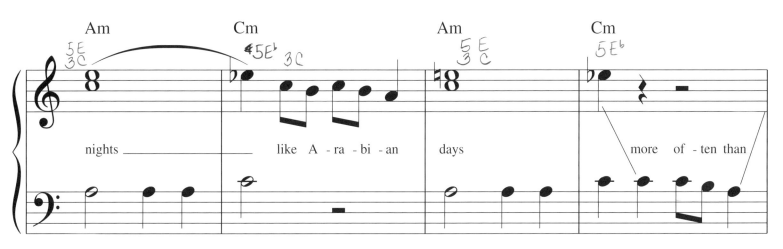

6

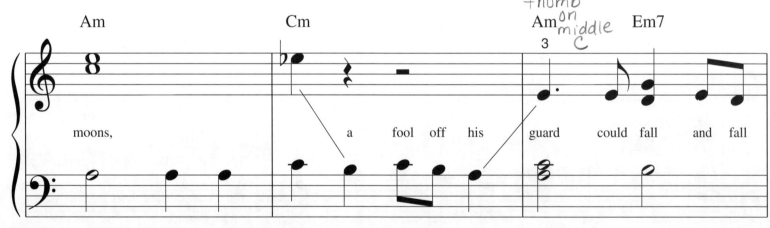

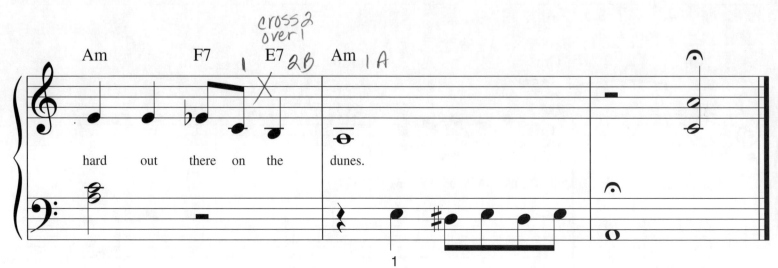

FRIEND LIKE ME
from Walt Disney's ALADDIN

Lyrics by HOWARD ASHMAN
Music by ALAN MENKEN

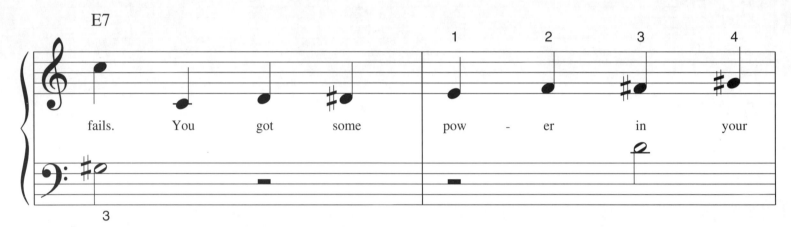

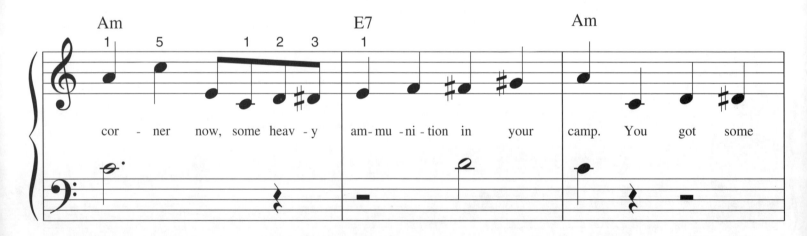

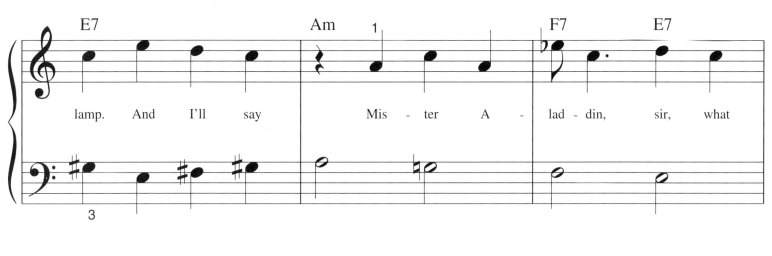

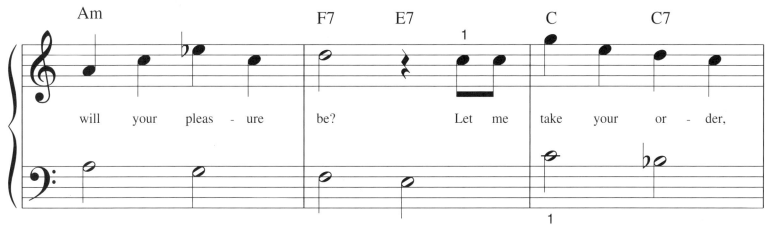

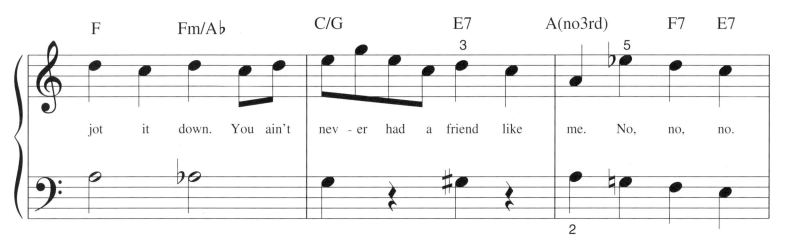

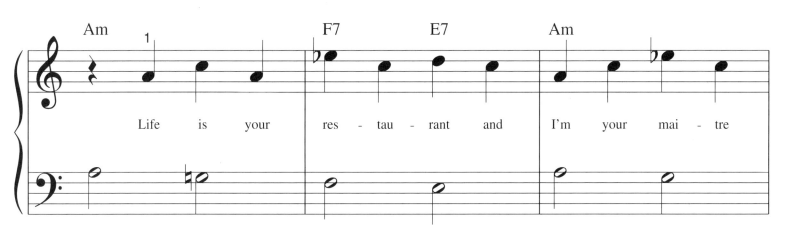

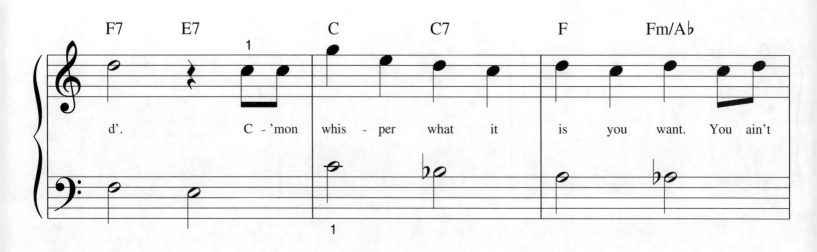

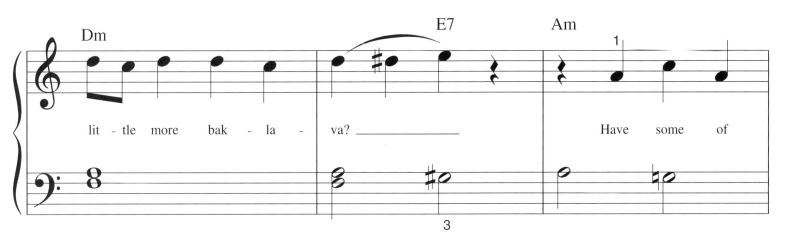

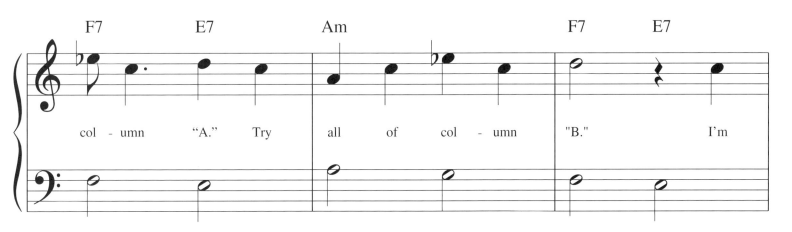

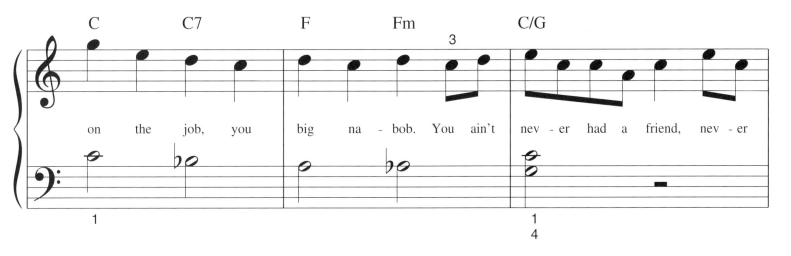

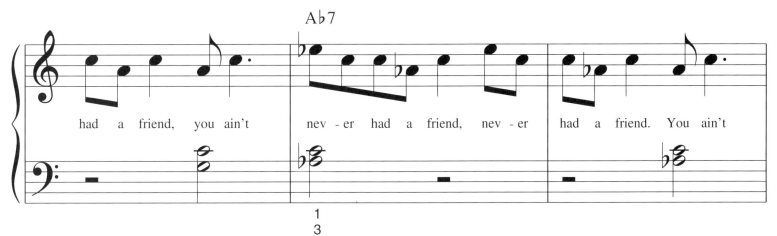

ONE JUMP AHEAD

from Walt Disney's ALADDIN

Music by ALAN MENKEN
Lyrics by TIM RICE

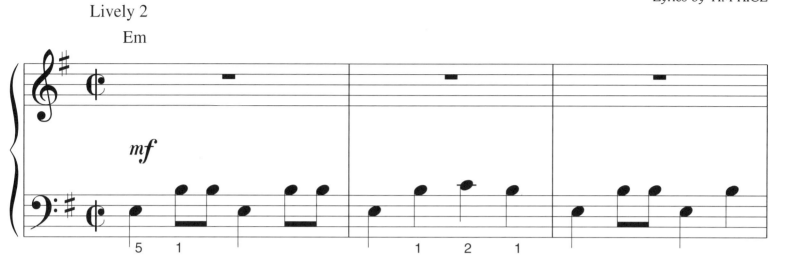

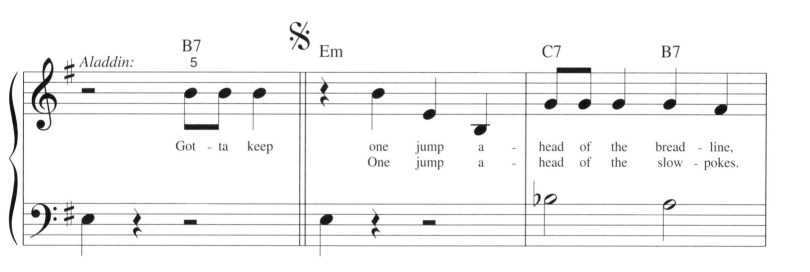

Got - ta keep one jump a - head of the bread - line,
One jump a - head of the slow - pokes.

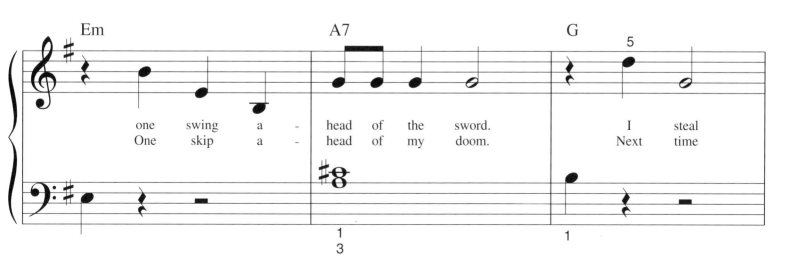

one swing a - head of the sword. I steal
One skip a - head of my doom. Next time

14

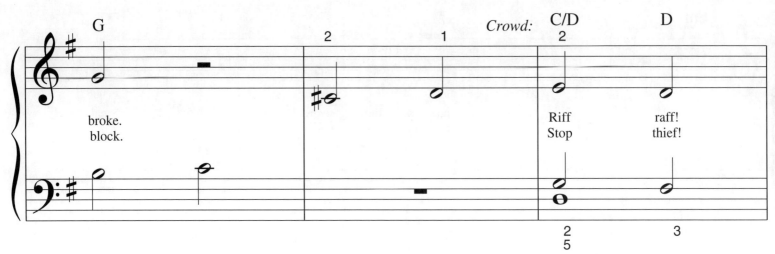

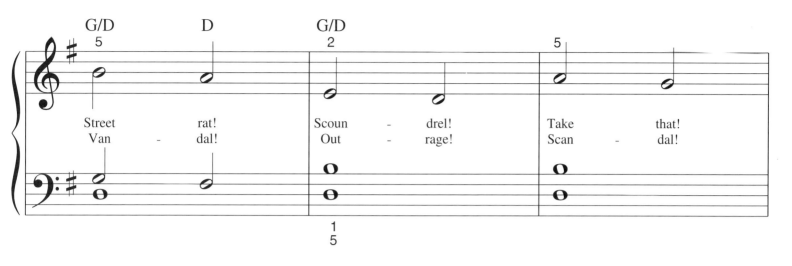

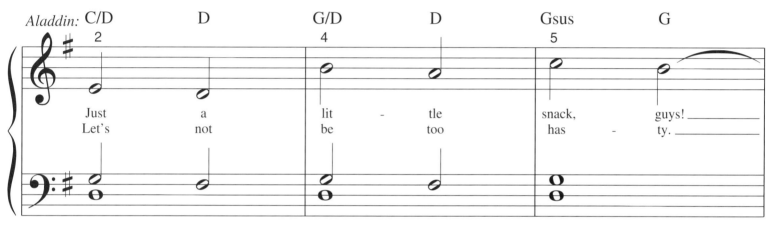

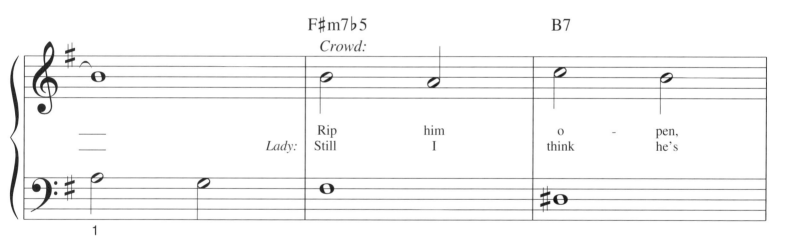

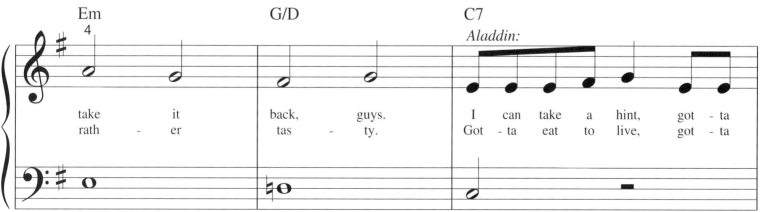

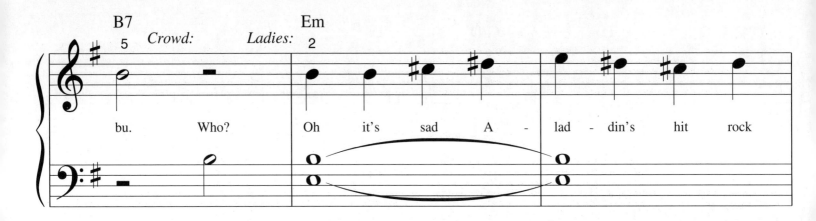

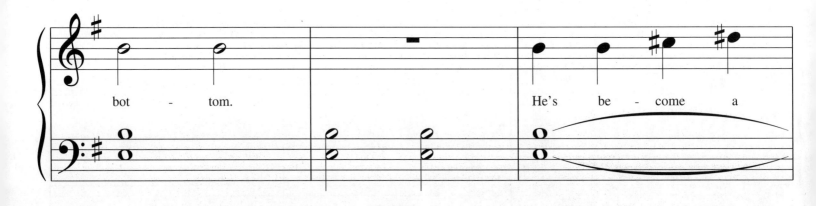

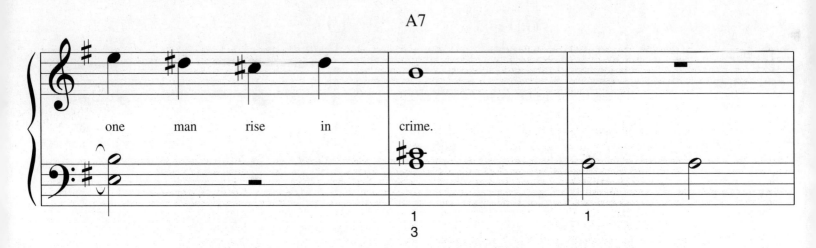

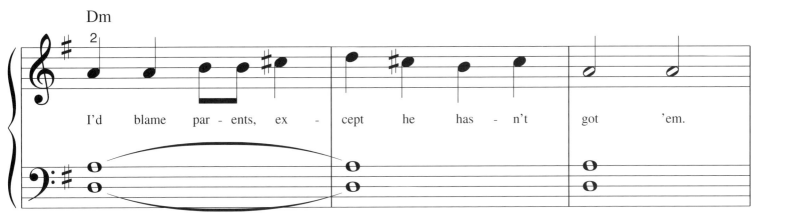

Dm

I'd blame par - ents, ex - cept he has - n't got 'em.

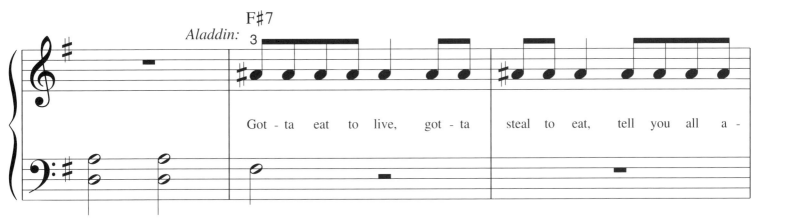

F#7

Aladdin:

Got - ta eat to live, got - ta steal to eat, tell you all a -

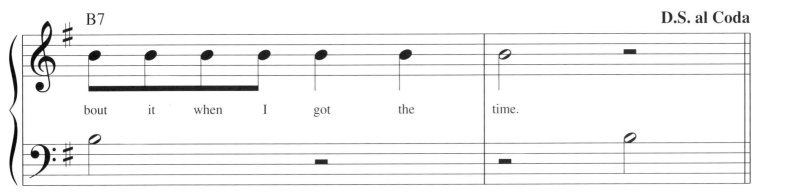

B7

D.S. al Coda

bout it when I got the time.

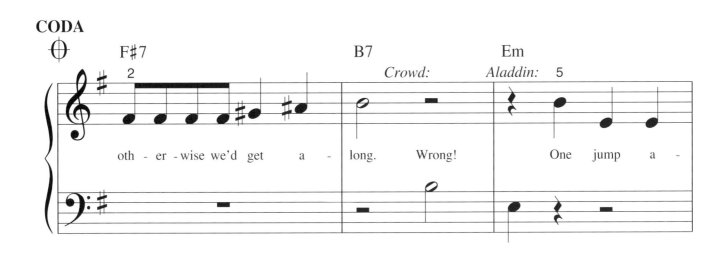

CODA

F#7

B7 Em

Crowd: *Aladdin:*

oth - er - wise we'd get a - long. Wrong! One jump a -

A WHOLE NEW WORLD

from Walt Disney's ALADDIN

Music by ALAN MENKEN
Lyrics by TIM RICE

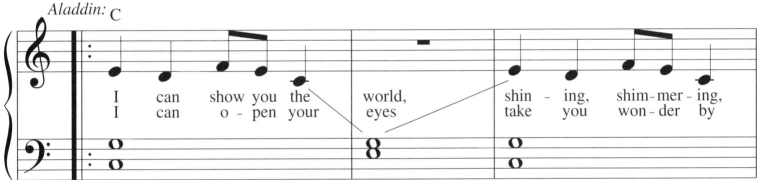

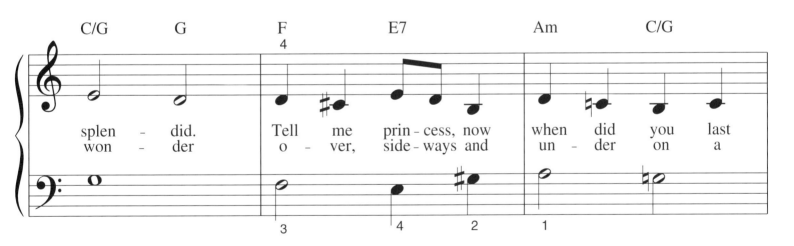

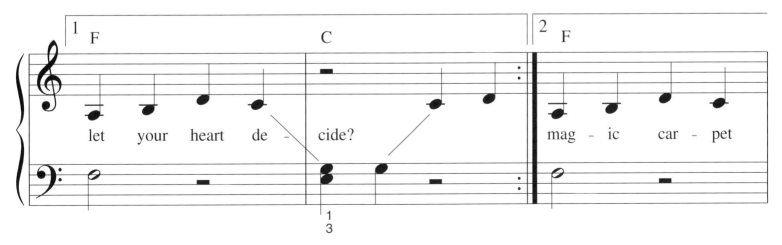

20

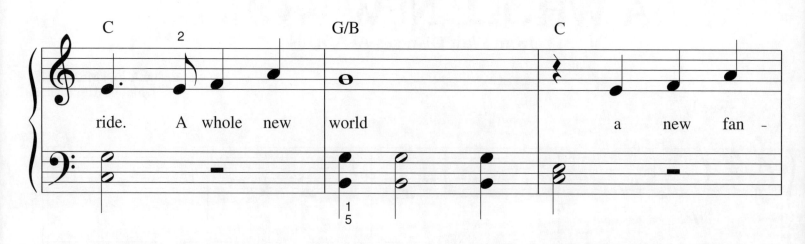

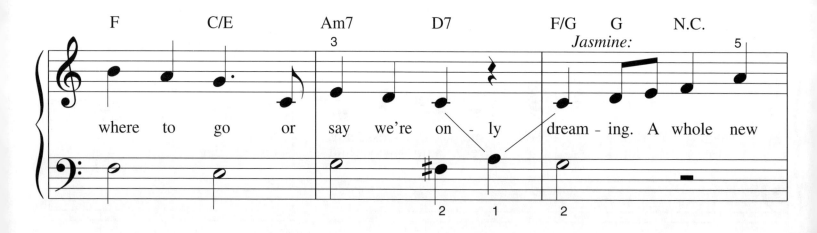

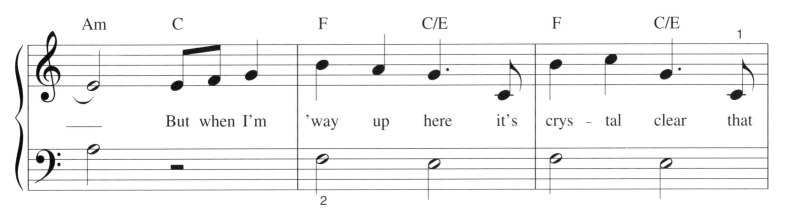

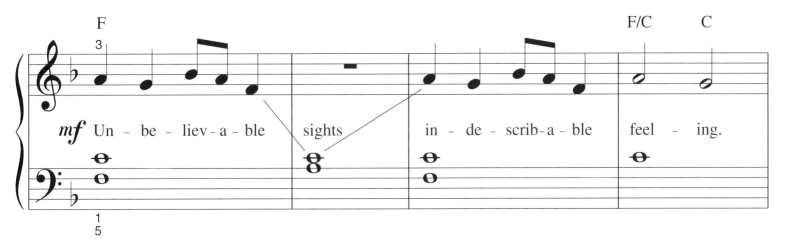

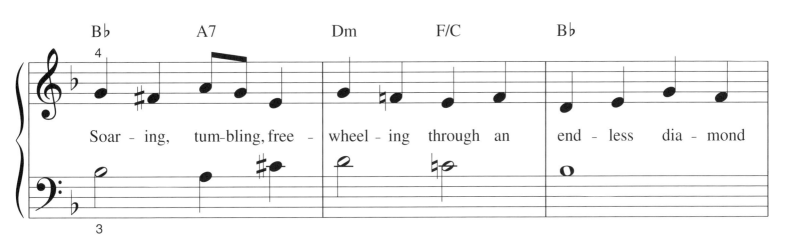

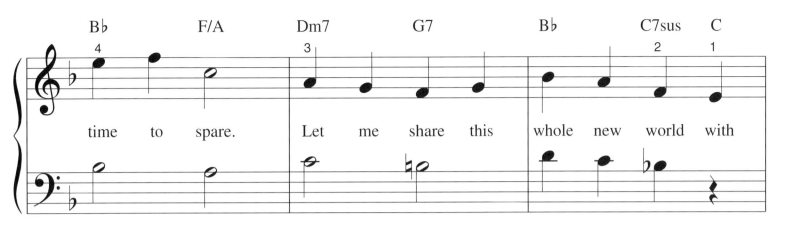

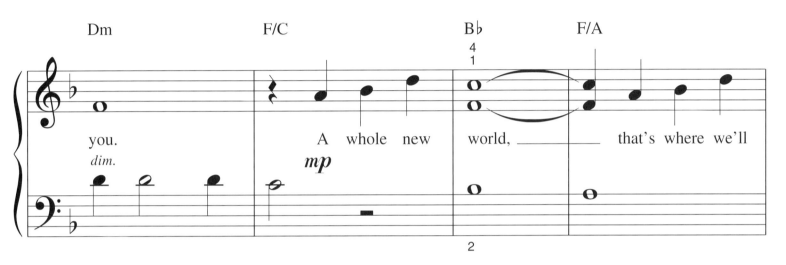

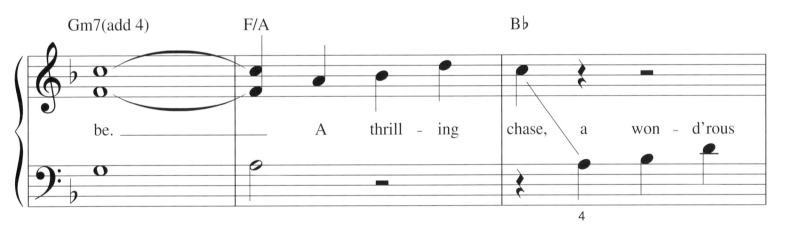

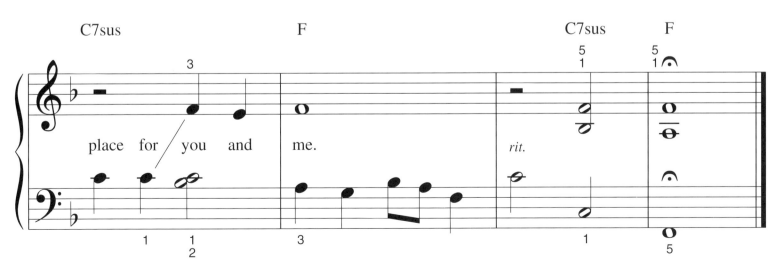

BE OUR GUEST

from Walt Disney's BEAUTY AND THE BEAST

Lyrics by HOWARD ASHMAN
Music by ALAN MENKEN

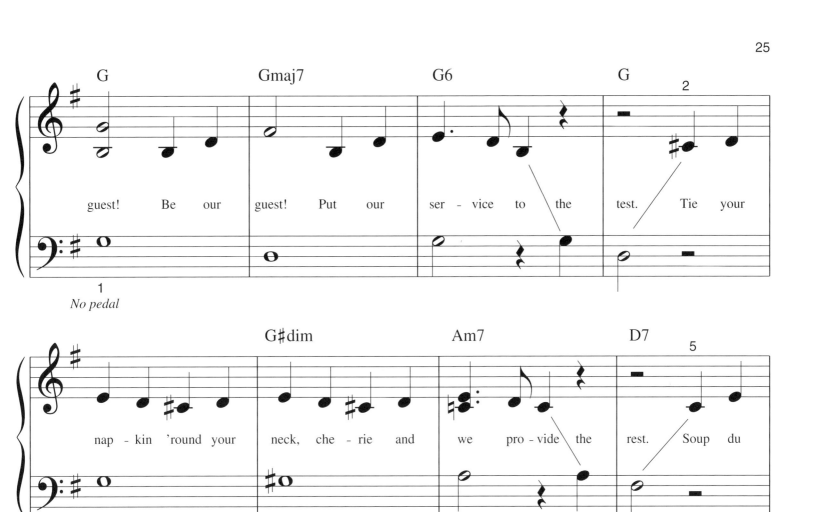

No pedal

G | Gmaj7 | G6 | G

guest! Be our guest! Put our ser - vice to the test. Tie your

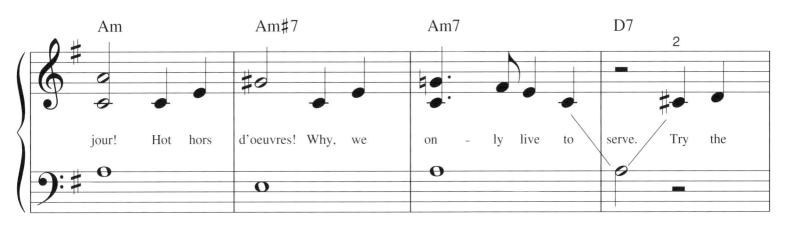

| G#dim | Am7 | D7

nap - kin 'round your neck, che - rie and we pro - vide the rest. Soup du

Am | Am#7 | Am7 | D7

jour! Hot hors d'oeuvres! Why, we on - ly live to serve. Try the

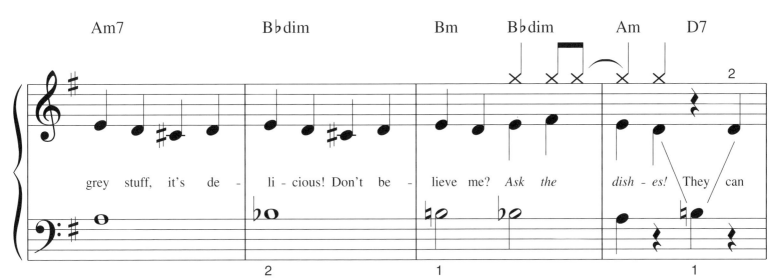

Am7 | B♭dim | Bm B♭dim | Am D7

grey stuff, it's de - li - cious! Don't be - lieve me? *Ask the dish - es!* They can

27

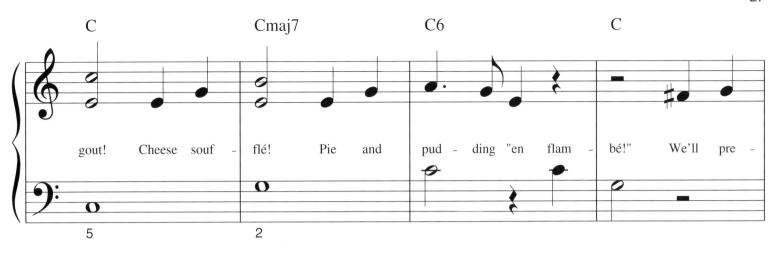

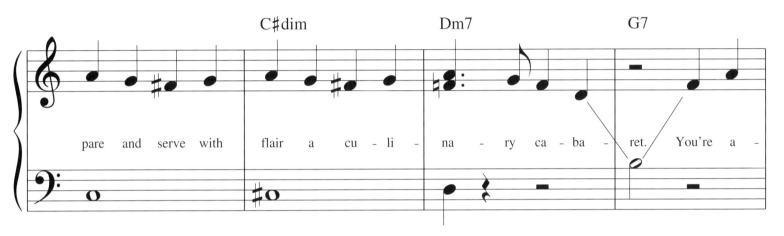

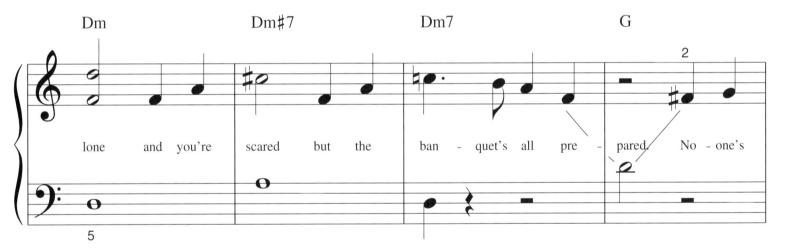

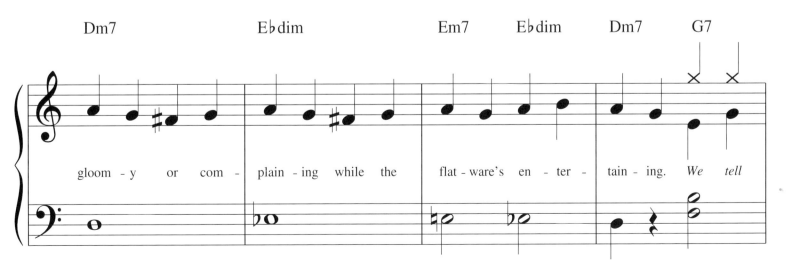

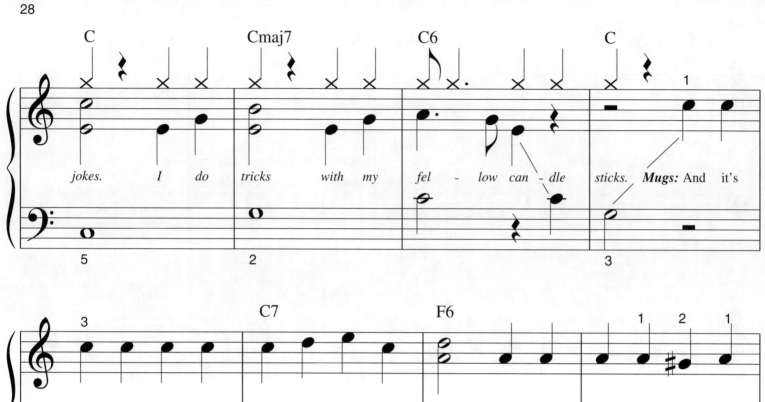

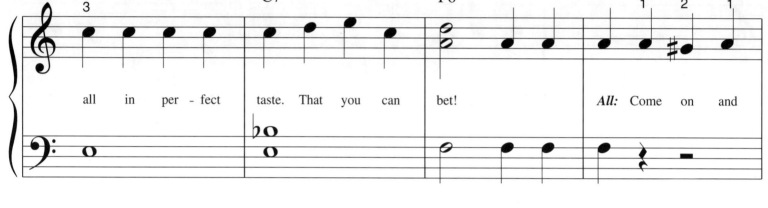

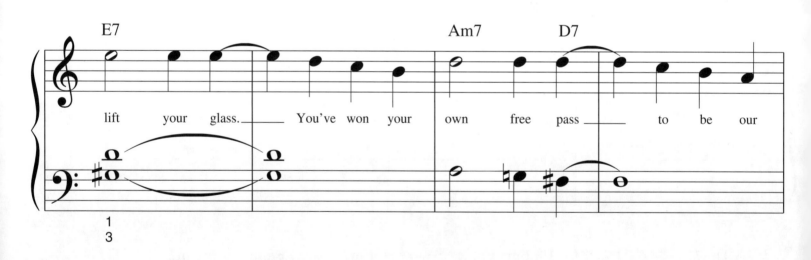

29

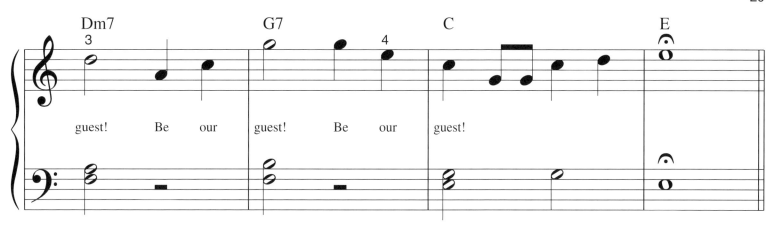

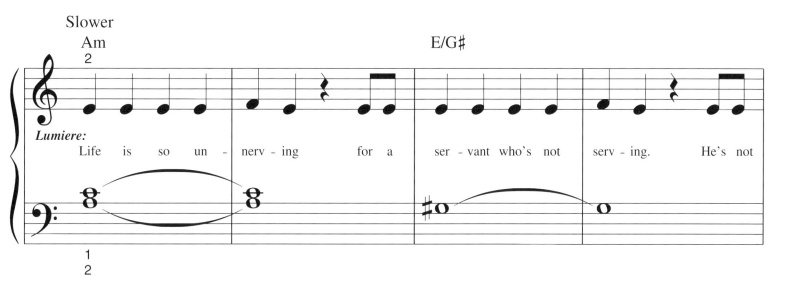

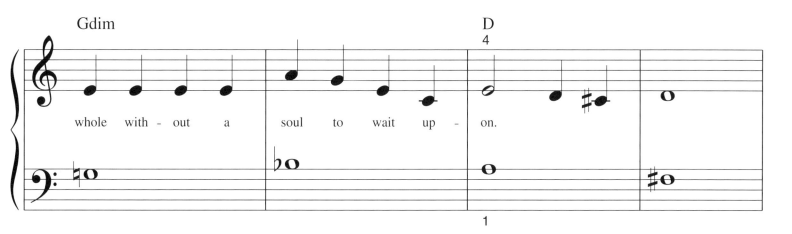

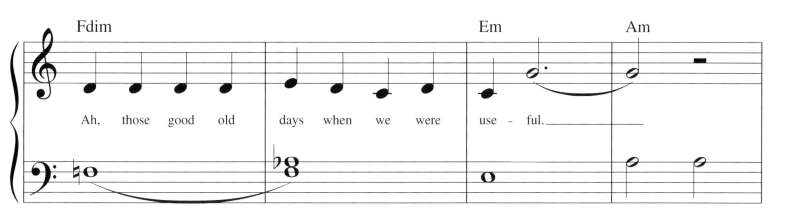

30

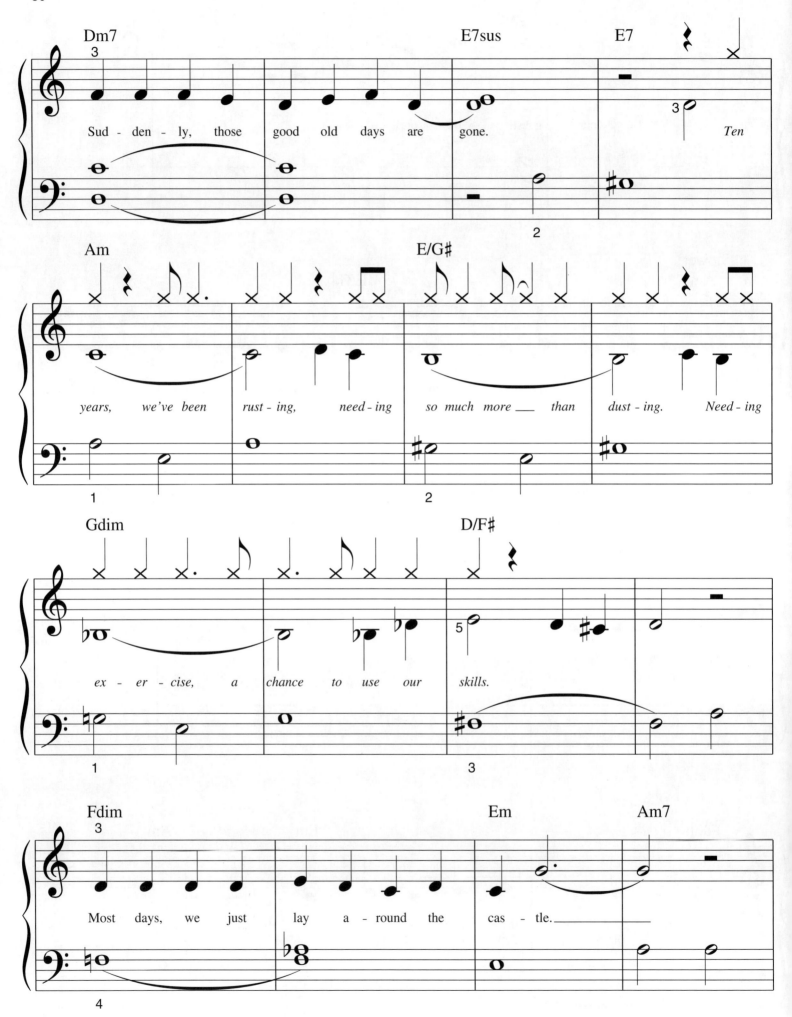

33

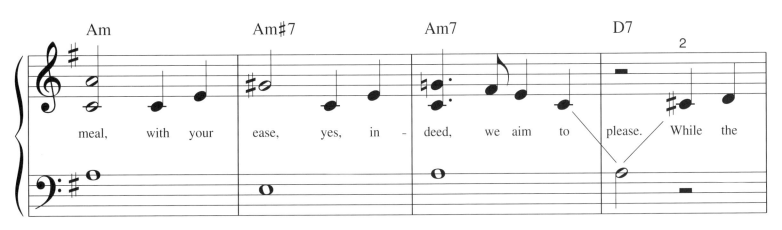

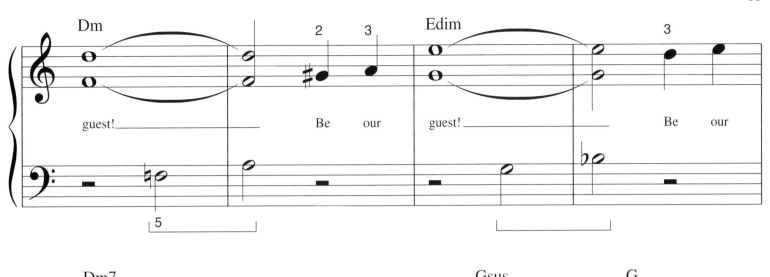

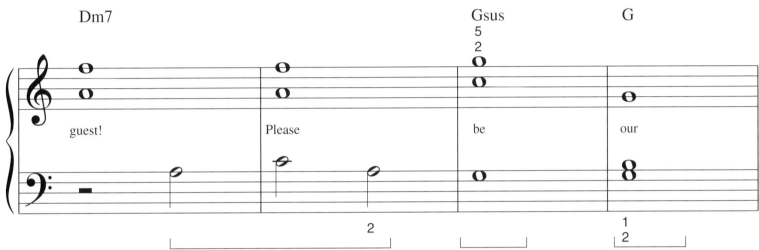

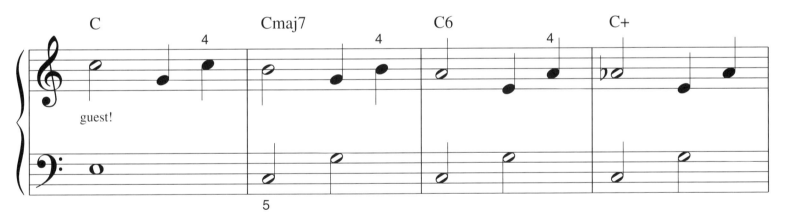

BEAUTY AND THE BEAST
from Walt Disney's BEAUTY AND THE BEAST

Lyrics by HOWARD ASHMAN
Music by ALAN MENKEN

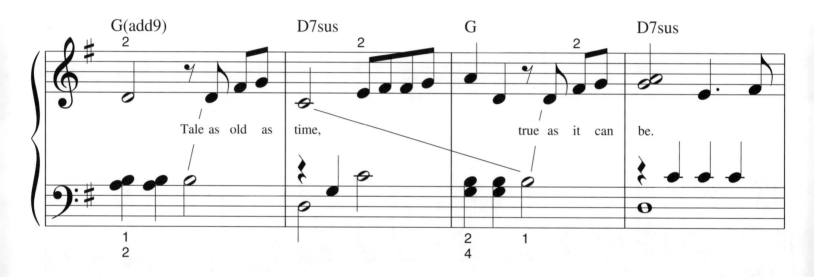

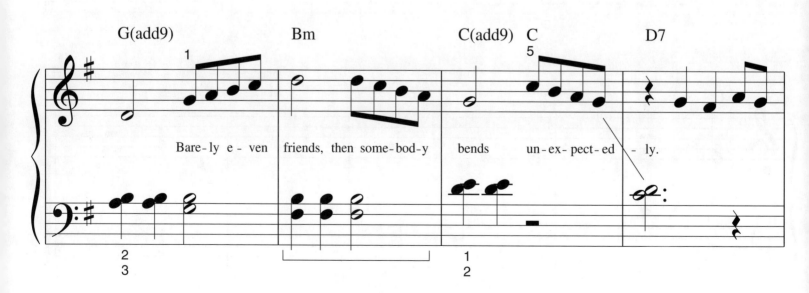

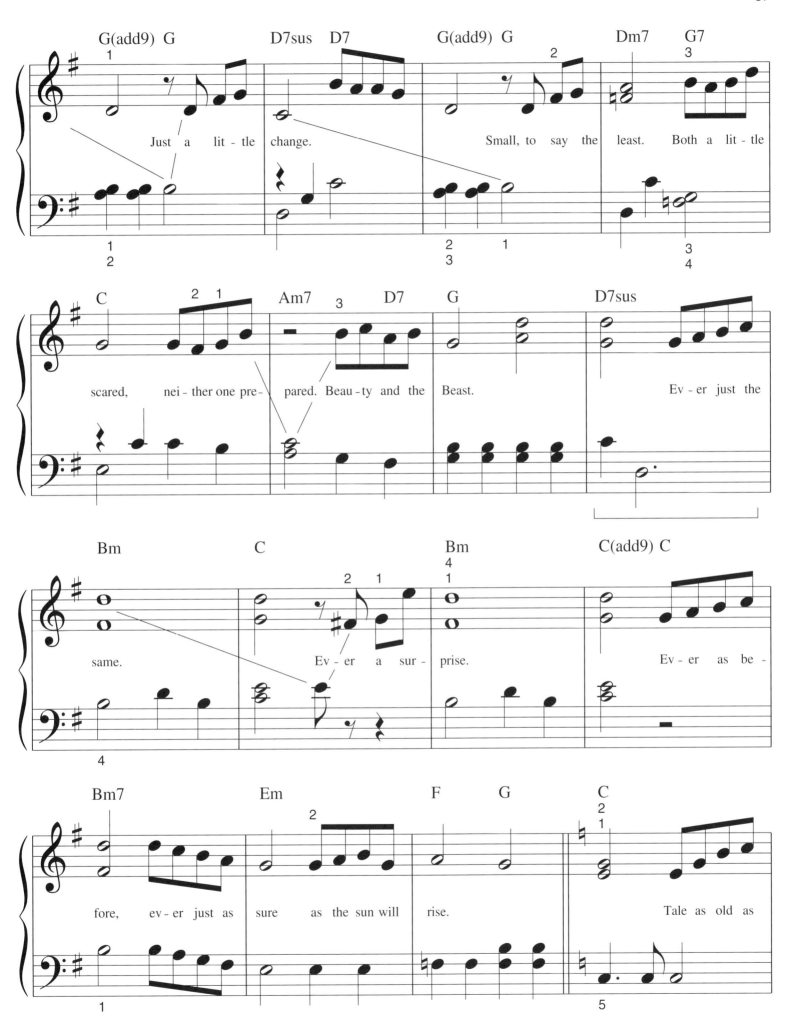

BELLE
from Walt Disney's BEAUTY AND THE BEAST

Lyrics by HOWARD ASHMAN
Music by ALAN MENKEN

Moderately slow

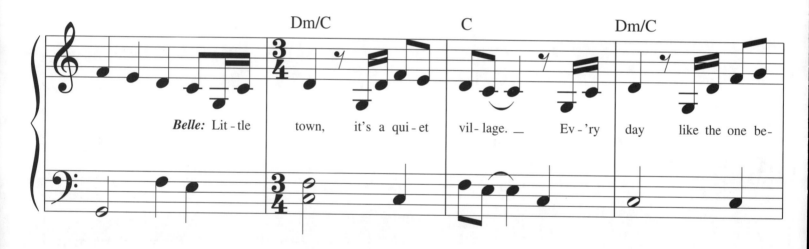

Belle: Lit-tle town, it's a qui-et vil-lage. __ Ev-'ry day like the one be-

fore. Lit-tle town full of lit-tle peo-ple wak-ing up to say: *Townsfolk:* Bon-

41

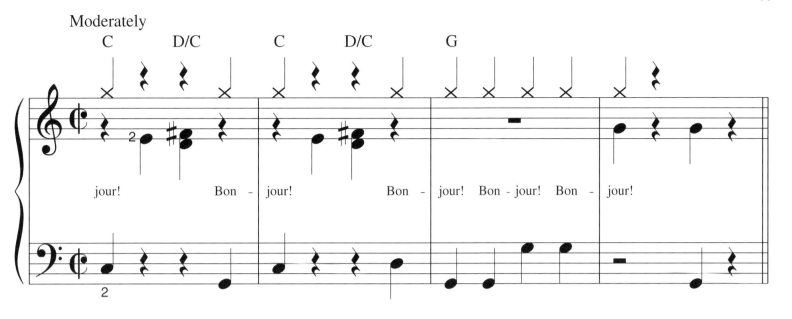

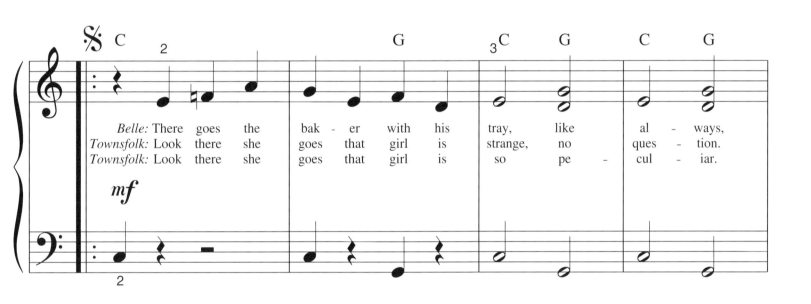

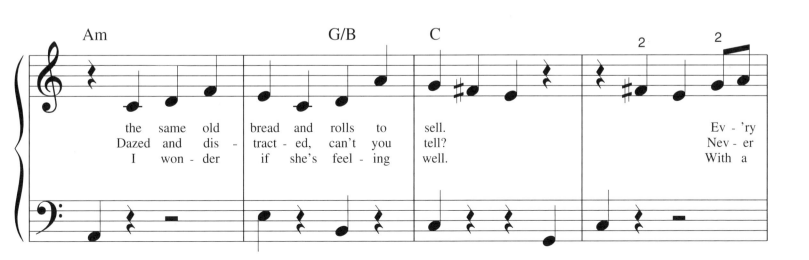

42

44

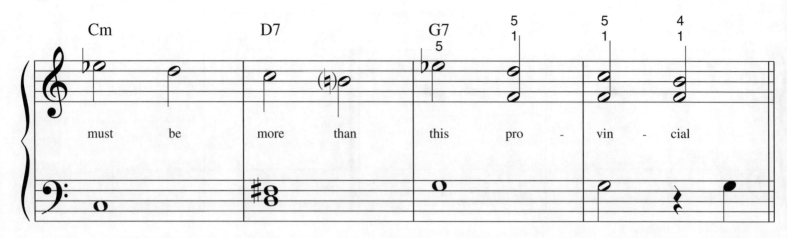

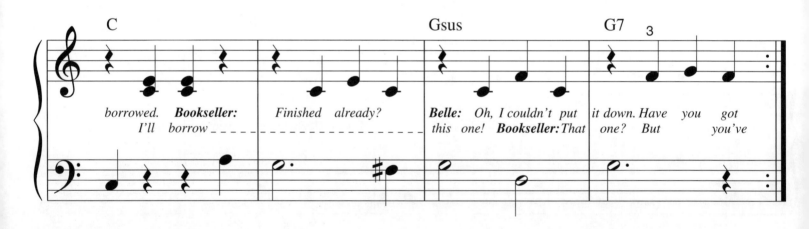

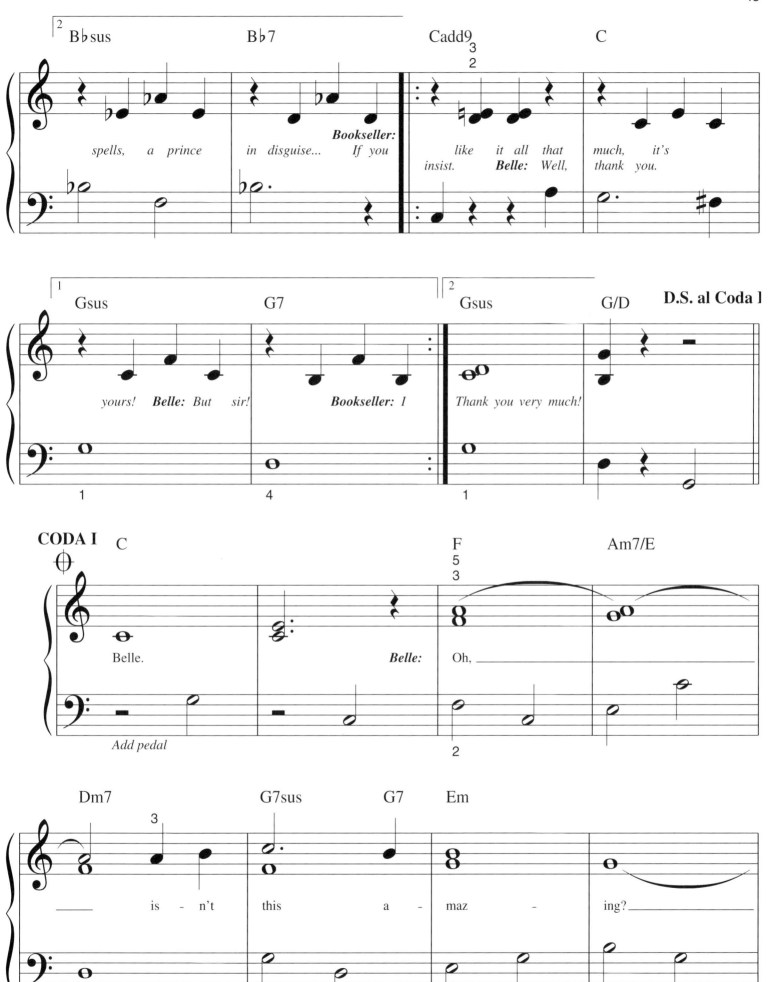

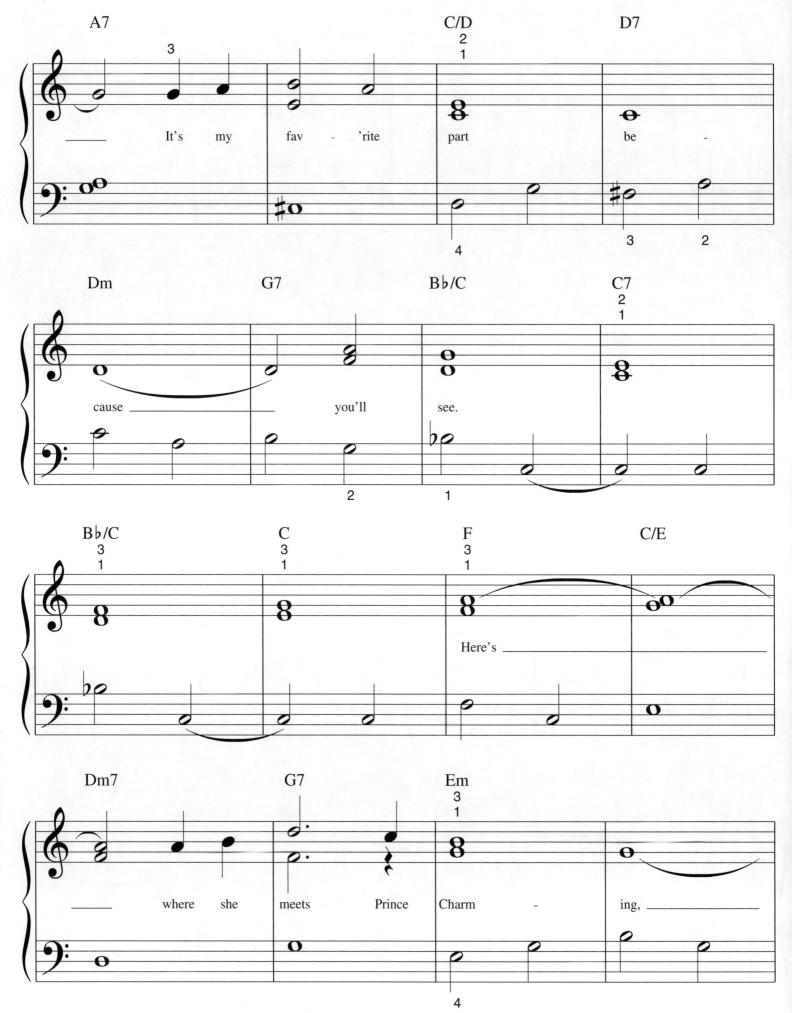

No Pedal

Woman: Now, it's no won – der that her
Townsfolk: Look there she goes a girl who's

name means "beau – ty."
strange but spe – cial.

Her looks have got no par – al –
A most pe – cu – liar mad – 'moi –

48

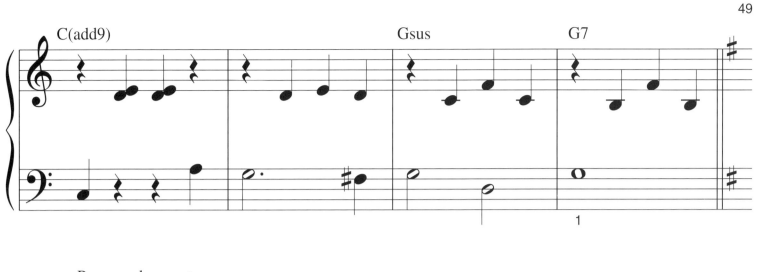

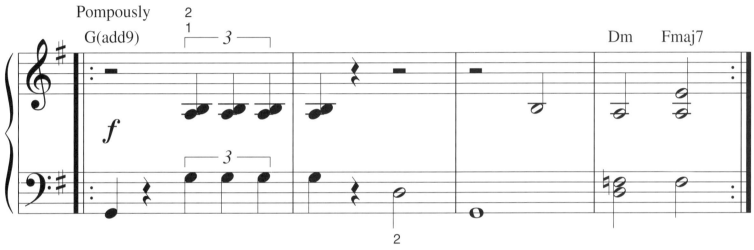

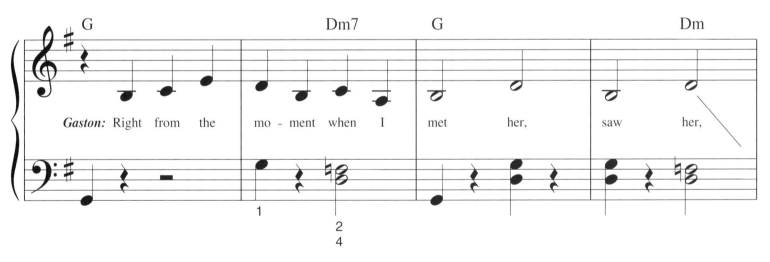

Gaston: Right from the mo - ment when I met her, saw her,

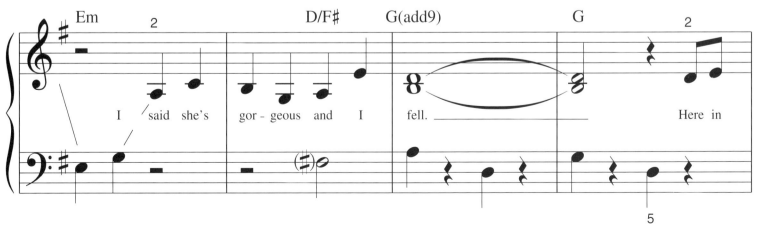

I said she's gor - geous and I fell. _____ Here in

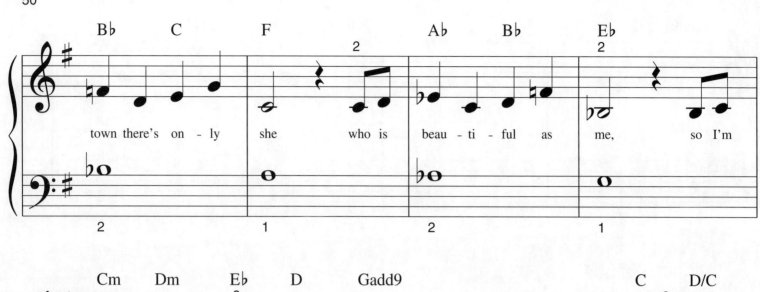

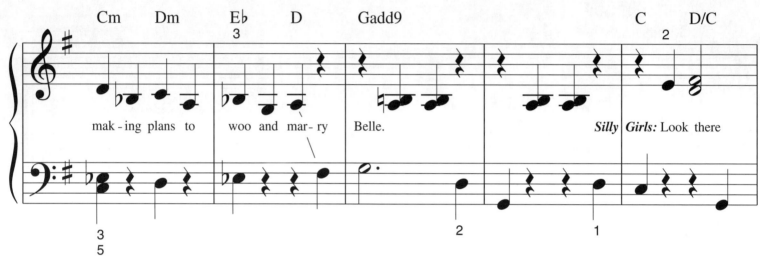

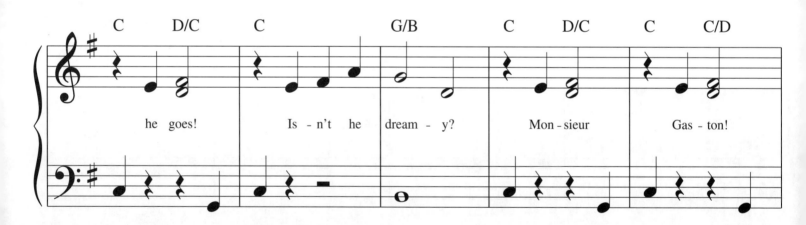

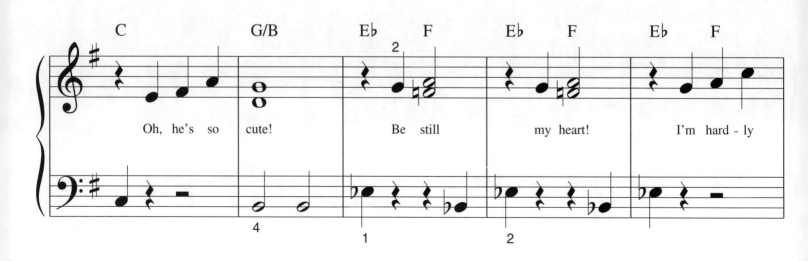

51

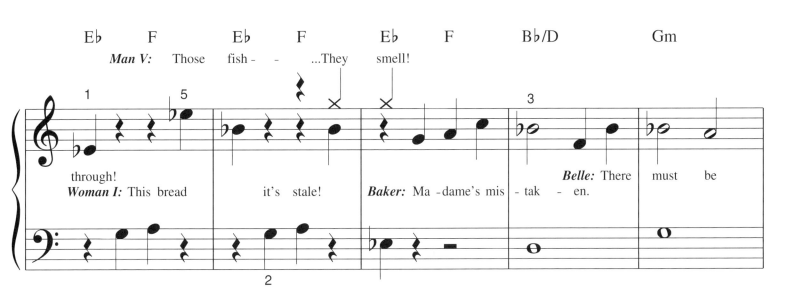

SOMETHING THERE
from Walt Disney's BEAUTY AND THE BEAST

Lyrics by HOWARD ASHMAN
Music by ALAN MENKEN

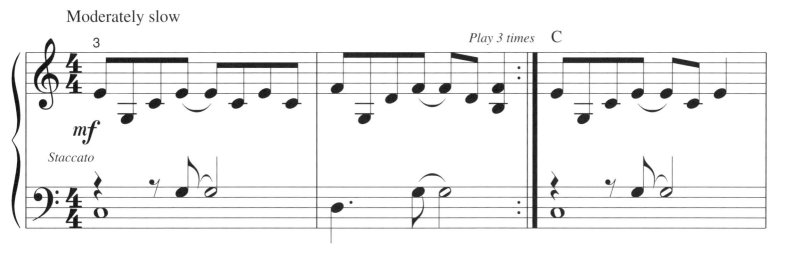

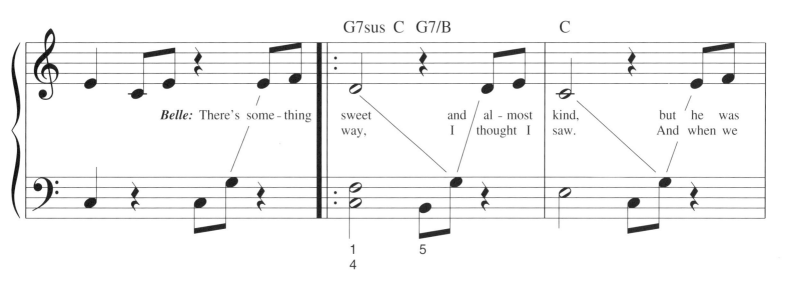

54

57

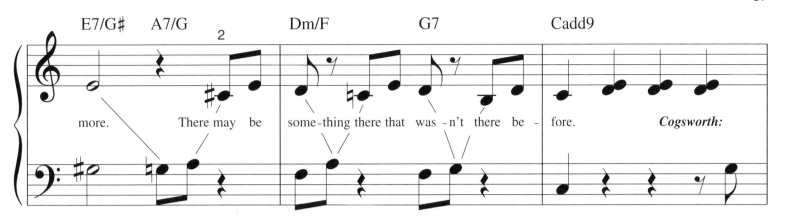

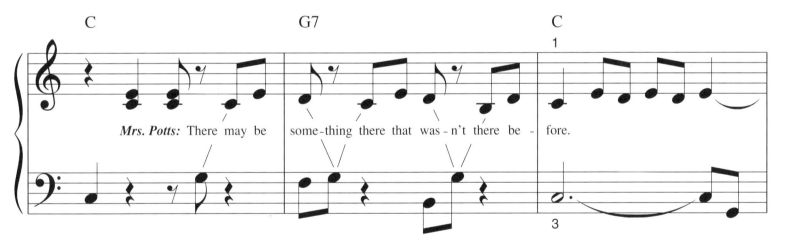

MY FUNNY FRIEND AND ME

from Walt Disney Pictures' THE EMPEROR'S NEW GROOVE

Lyrics by STING
Music by STING and DAVID HARTLEY

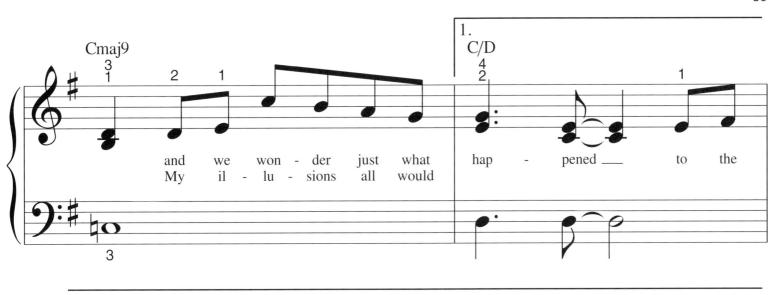

and we won - der just what hap - pened ___ to the
My il - lu - sions all would

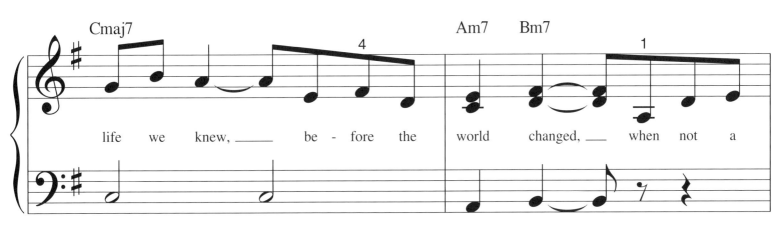

life we knew, ___ be - fore the world changed, ___ when not a

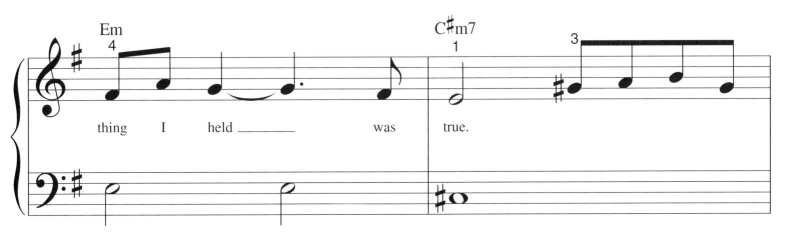

thing I held _____ was true.

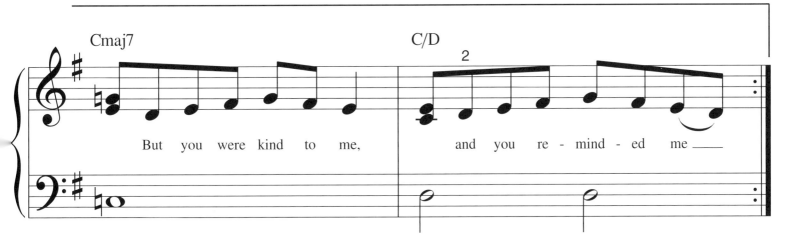

But you were kind to me, and you re - mind - ed me ___

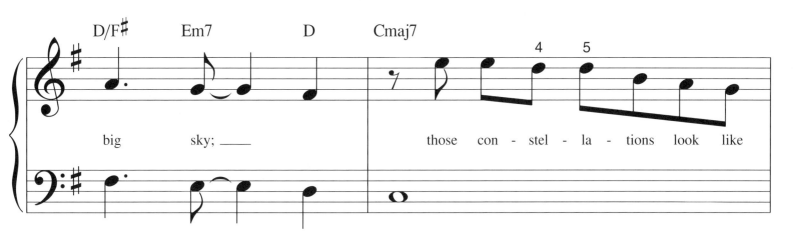

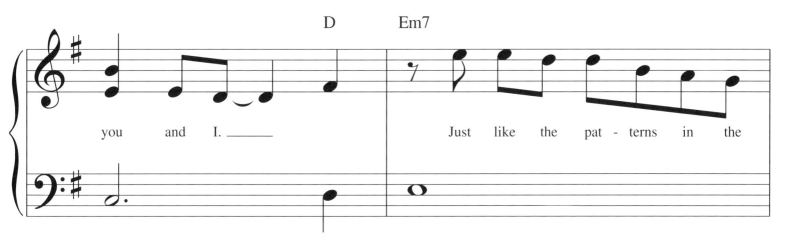

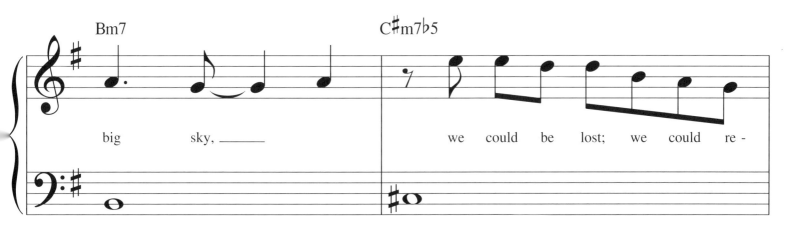

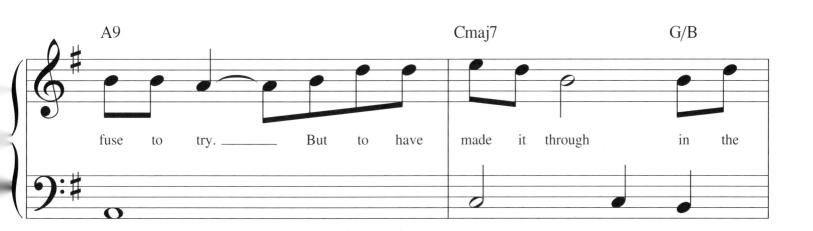

62

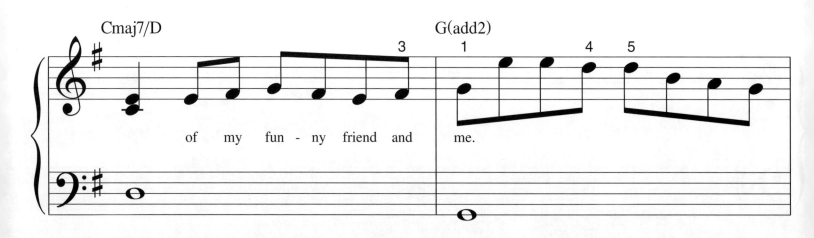

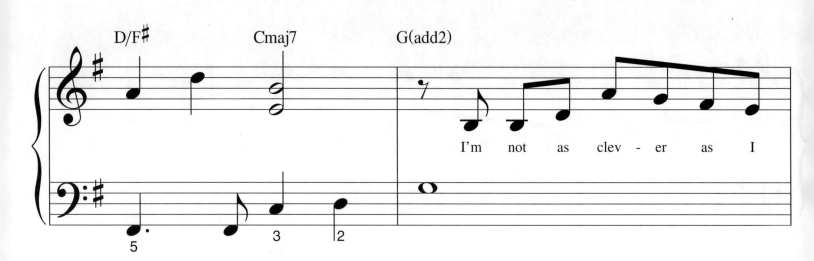

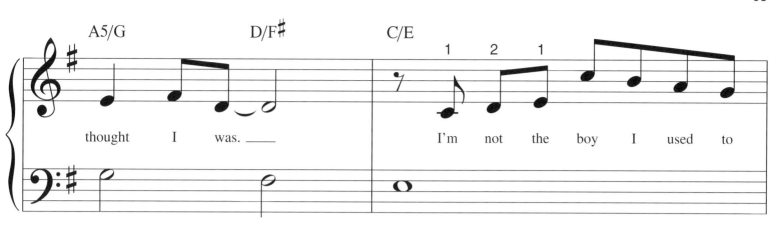

A5/G   D/F#   C/E

thought I was. ____   I'm not the boy I used to

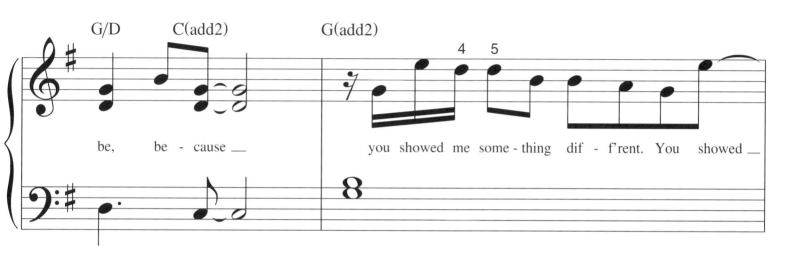

G/D   C(add2)   G(add2)

be,   be - cause ___   you showed me some - thing dif - f'rent. You showed __

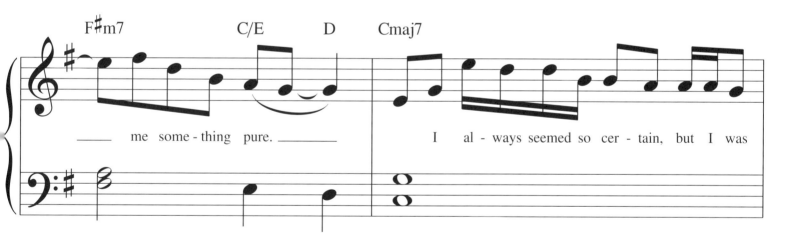

F#m7   C/E   D   Cmaj7

___ me some - thing pure. _____   I al - ways seemed so cer - tain, but I was

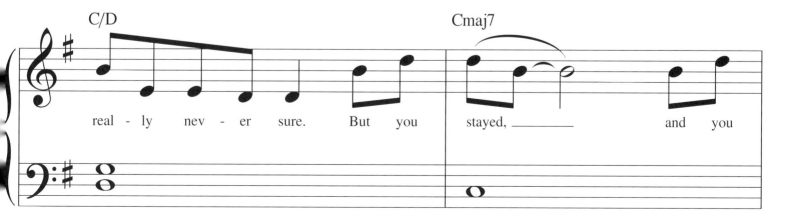

C/D   Cmaj7

real - ly nev - er sure. But you   stayed, _____ and you

called my name ___   when oth - ers would have walked out on a lou - sy

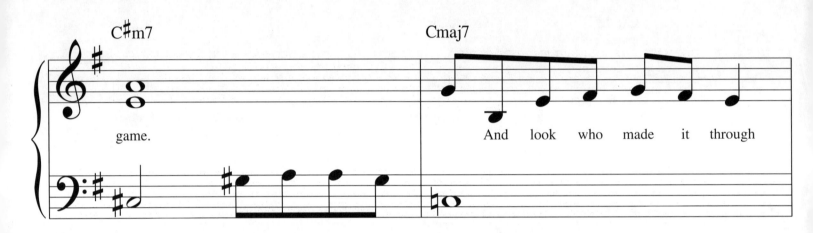

game.   And look who made it through

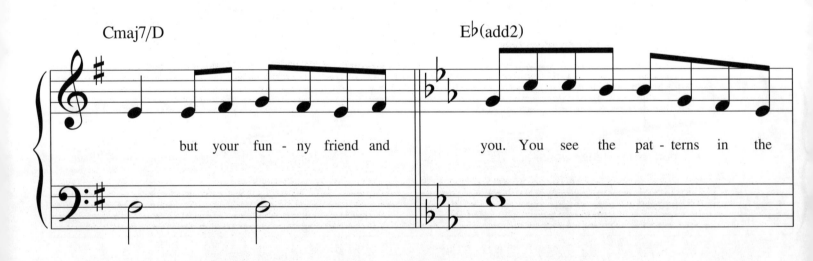

but your fun - ny friend and   you. You see the pat - terns in the

big sky. ___   Those con - stel - la - tions look like

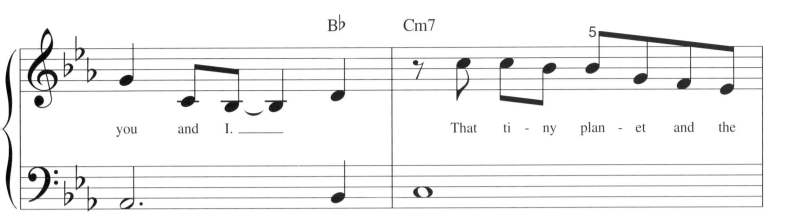

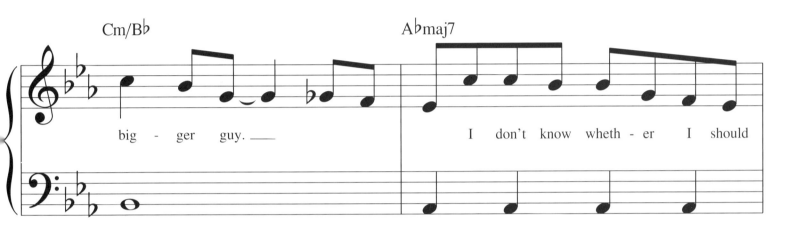

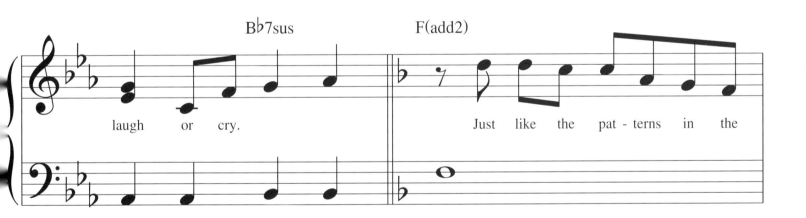

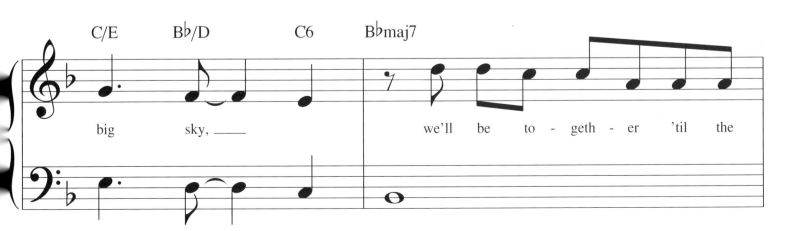

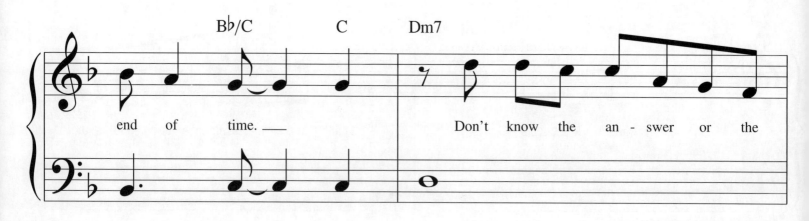

end of time. ____ Don't know the an - swer or the

rea - son why. ____ We'll stick to - geth - er 'til the

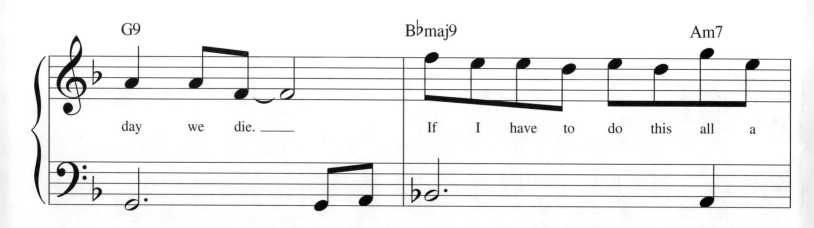

day we die. ____ If I have to do this all a

sec - ond time, ____ I won't com - plain or make a

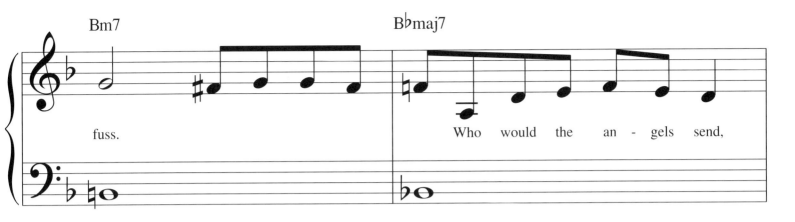

Bm7   B♭maj7

fuss.   Who would the an - gels send,

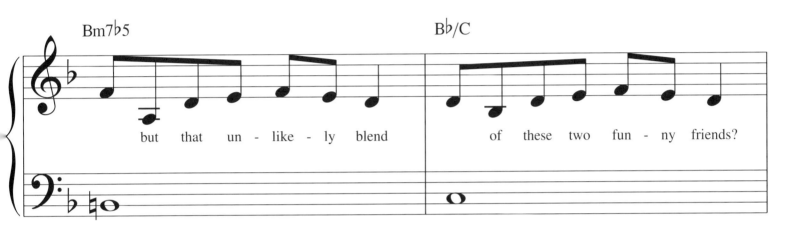

Bm7♭5   B♭/C

but that un - like - ly blend   of these two fun - ny friends?

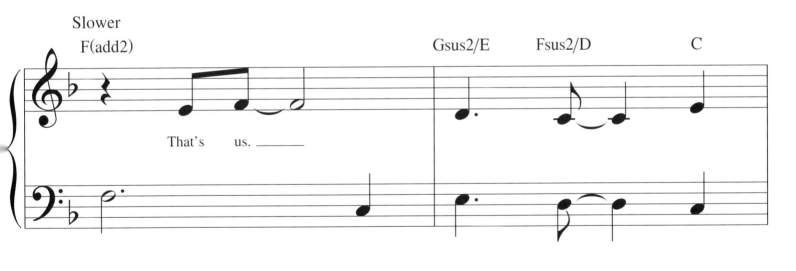

Slower
F(add2)   Gsus2/E   Fsus2/D   C

That's us. _____

B♭maj9   C7sus   F(add2)

GO THE DISTANCE

from Walt Disney Pictures' HERCULES

Music by ALAN MENKEN
Lyrics by DAVID ZIPPEL

Young Hercules: I have

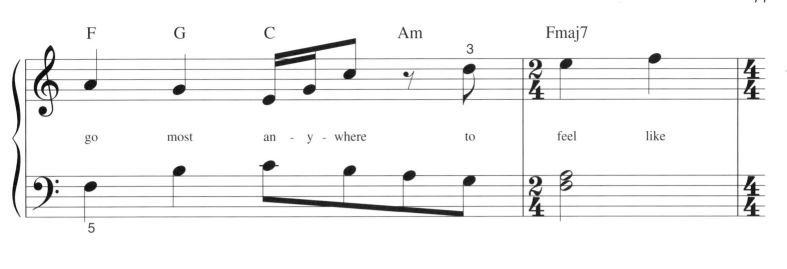

F G C Am Fmaj7

go most an - y - where to feel like

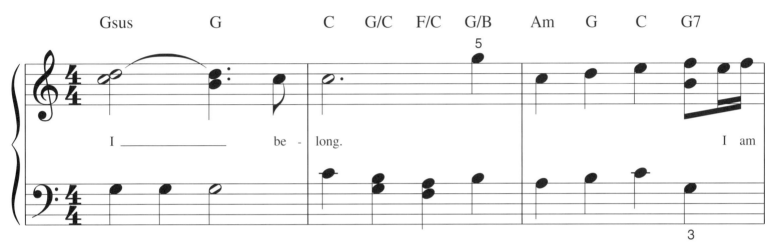

Gsus G C G/C F/C G/B Am G C G7

I _____ be - long. I am

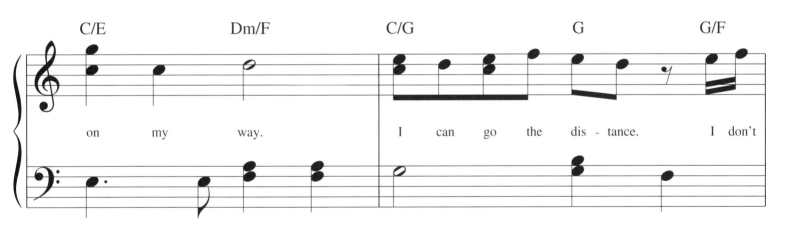

C/E Dm/F C/G G G/F

on my way. I can go the dis - tance. I don't

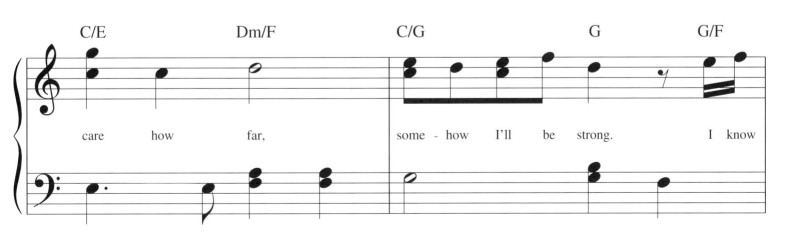

C/E Dm/F C/G G G/F

care how far, some - how I'll be strong. I know

I WON'T SAY
(I'm in Love)
from Walt Disney Pictures' HERCULES

Music by ALAN MENKEN
Lyrics by DAVID ZIPPEL

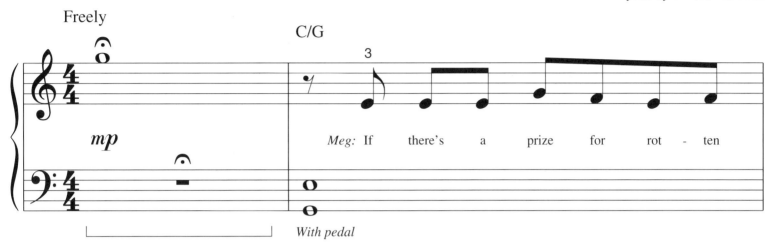

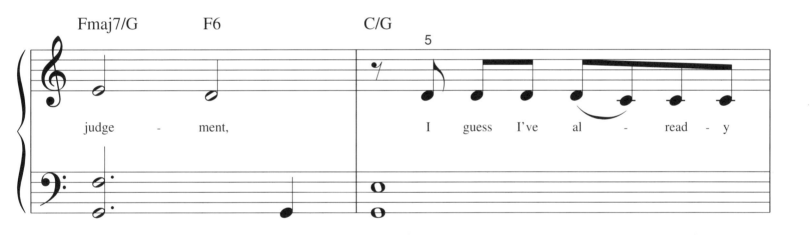

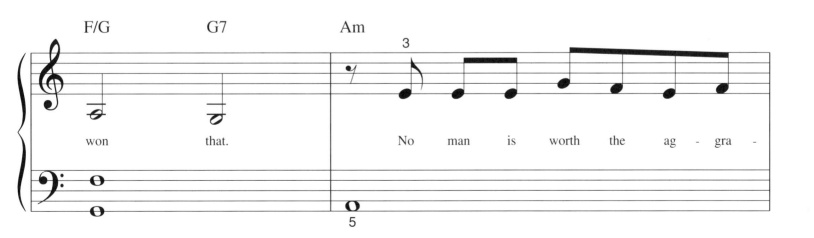

Moderate Rock

No pedal

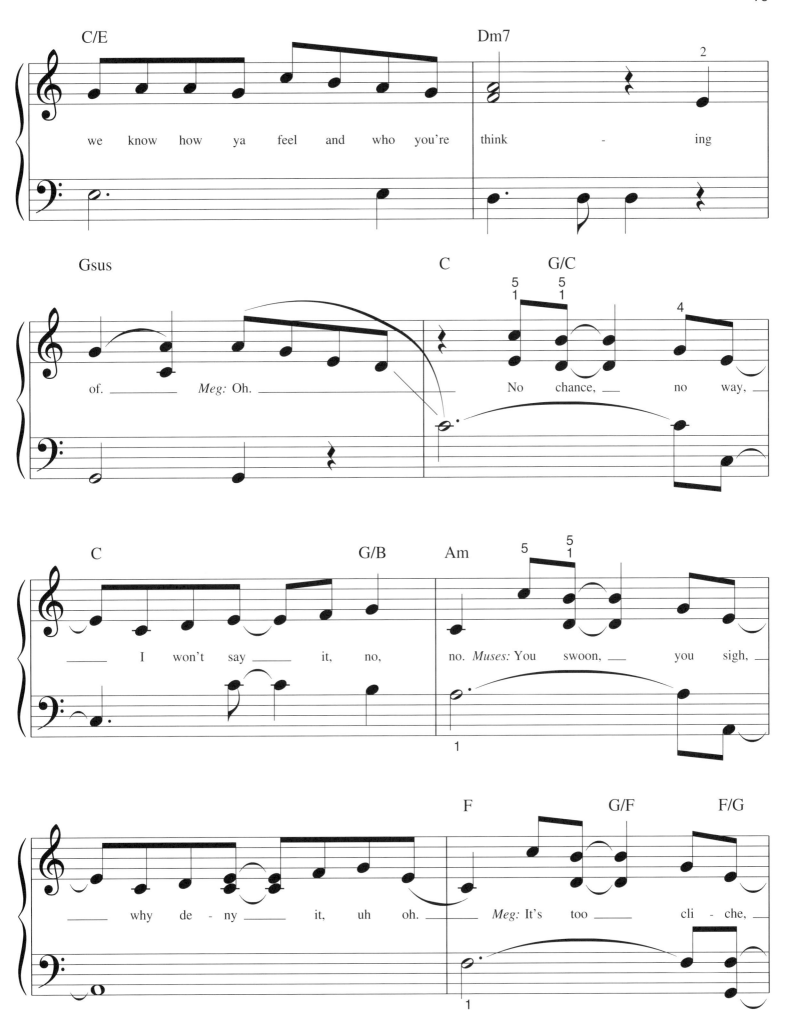

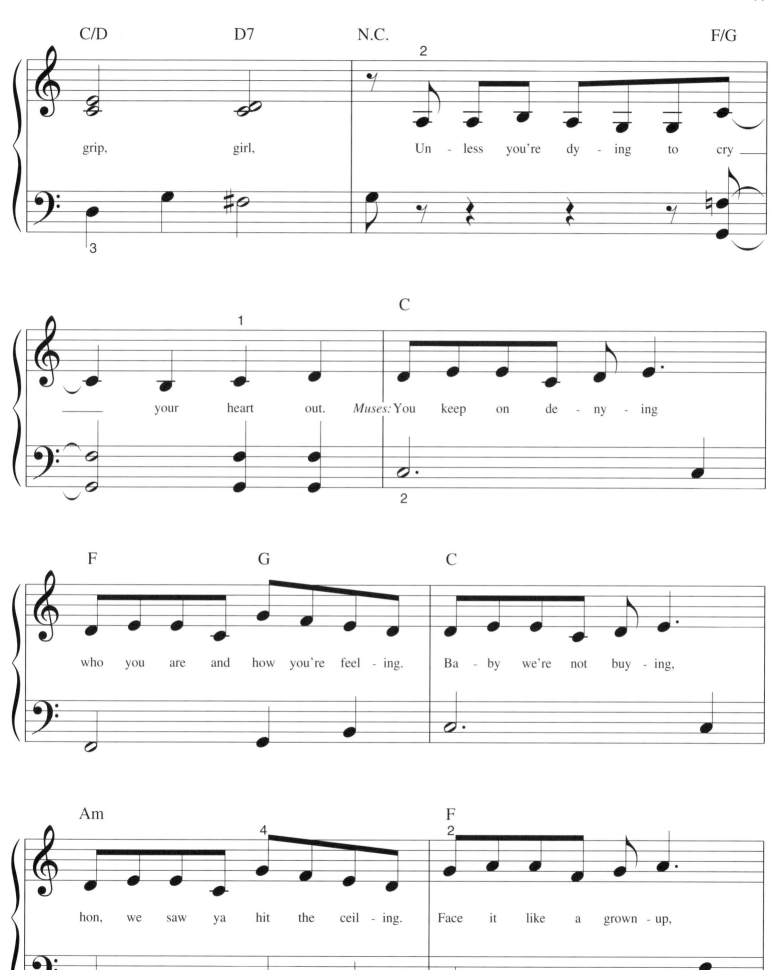

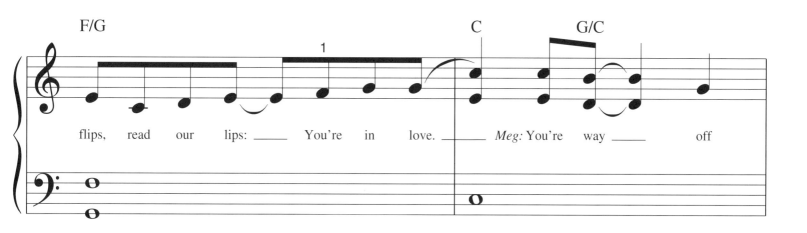

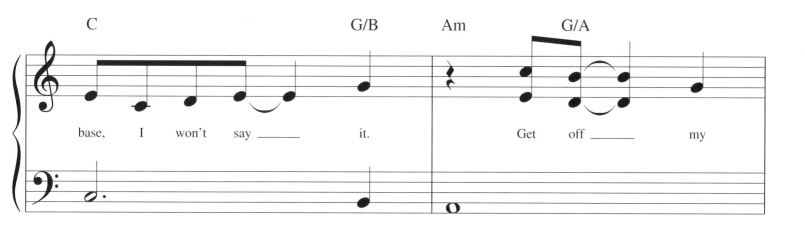

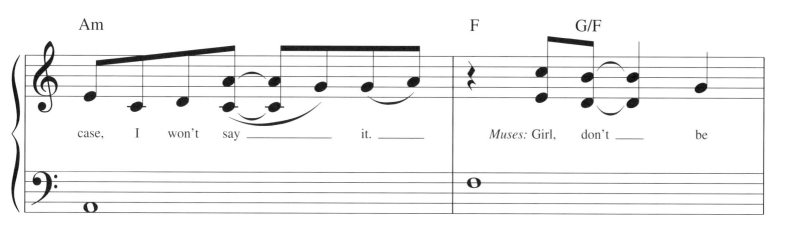

ZERO TO HERO
from Walt Disney Pictures' HERCULES

Music by ALAN MENKEN
Lyrics by DAVID ZIPPEL

THE COURT OF MIRACLES

from Walt Disney's THE HUNCHBACK OF NOTRE DAME

Music by ALAN MENKEN
Lyrics by STEPHEN SCHWARTZ

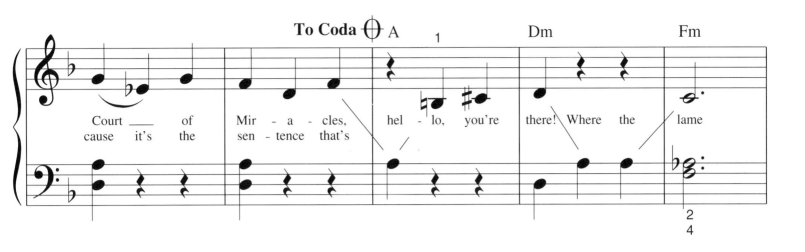

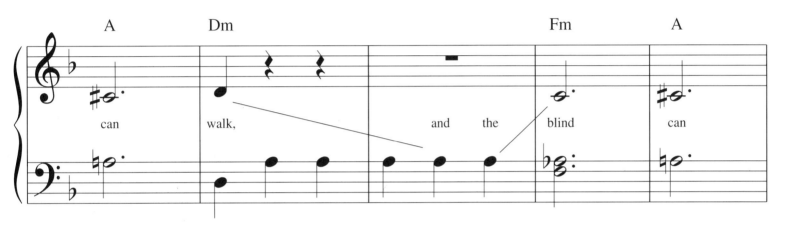

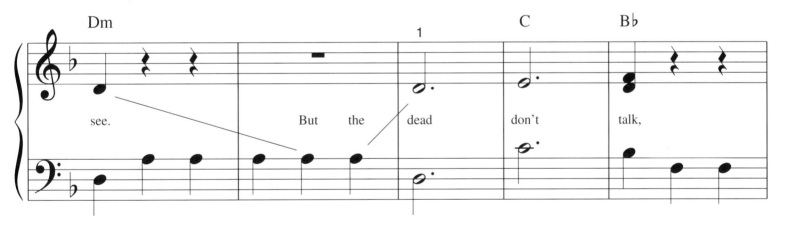

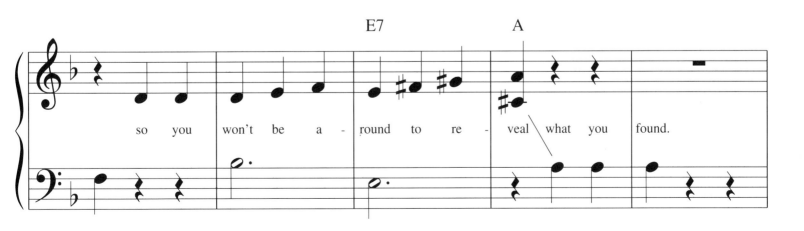

We have a meth - od for spies and in - trud - ers,

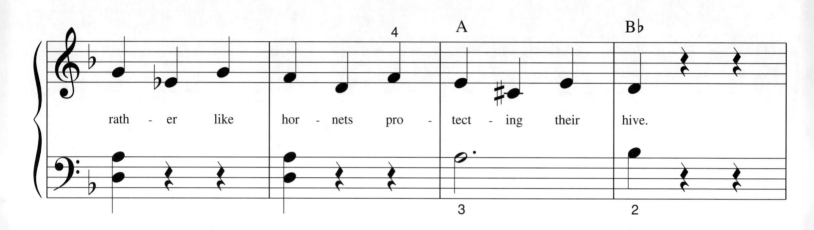

rath - er like hor - nets pro - tect - ing their hive.

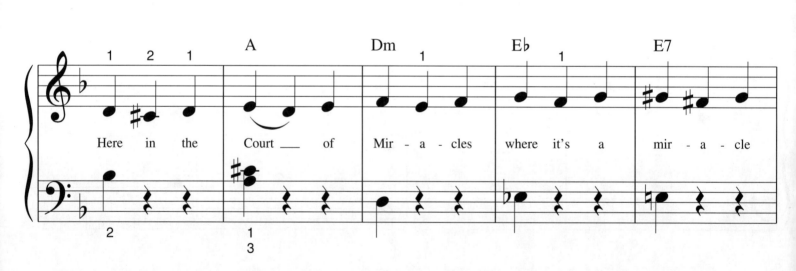

Here in the Court ___ of Mir - a - cles where it's a mir - a - cle

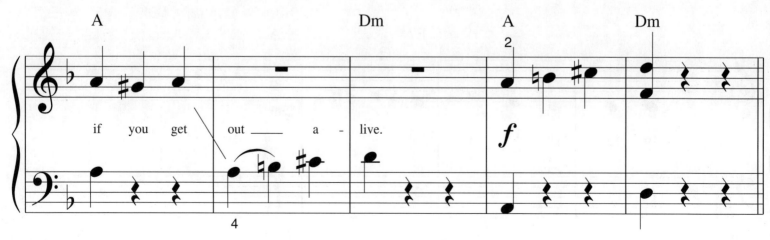

if you get out ___ a - live.

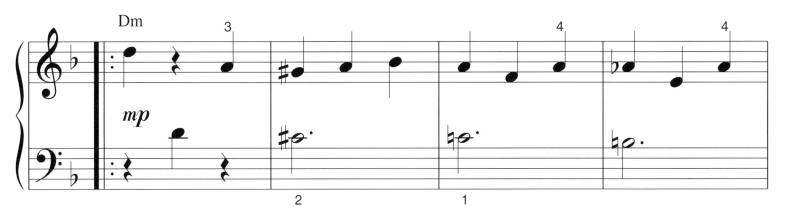

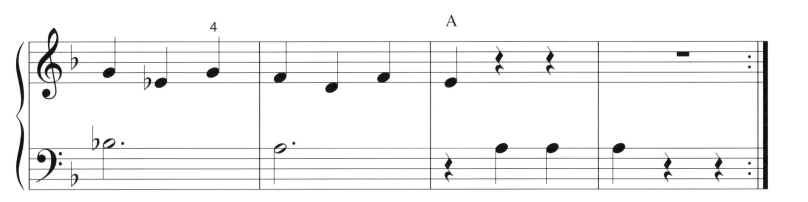

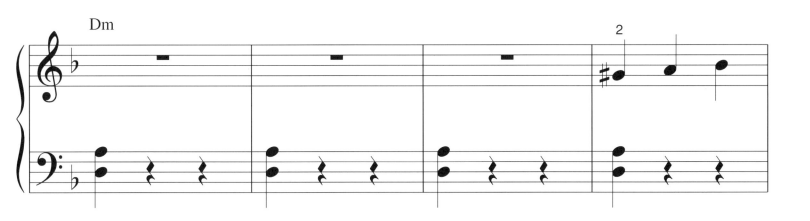

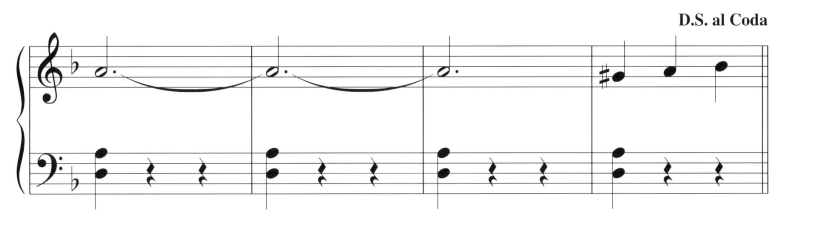

GOD HELP THE OUTCASTS

from Walt Disney's THE HUNCHBACK OF NOTRE DAME

Music by ALAN MENKEN
Lyrics by STEPHEN SCHWARTZ

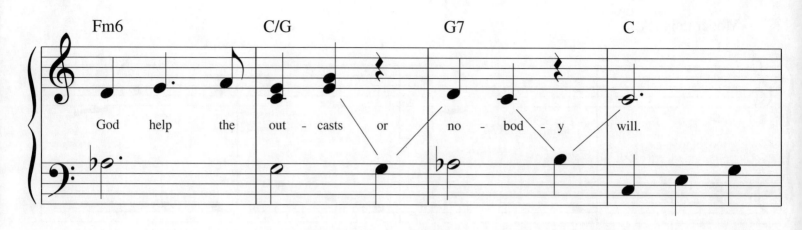

God help the out - casts or no - bod - y will.

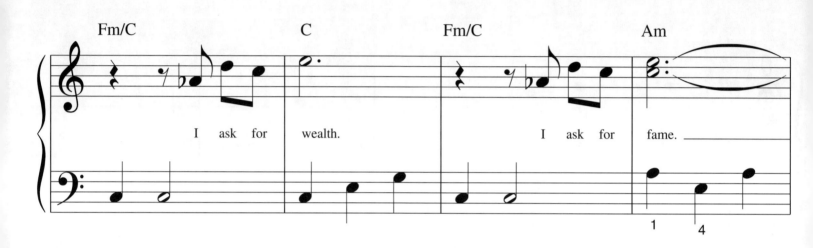

I ask for wealth. I ask for fame. ___

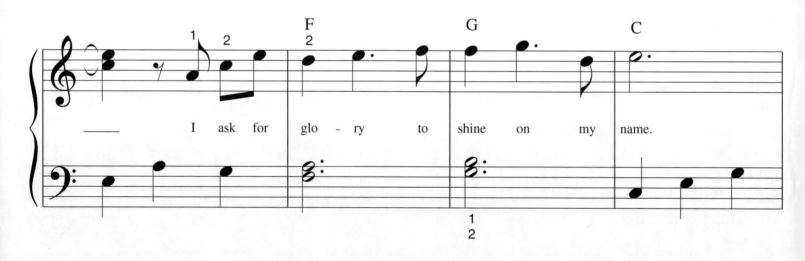

___ I ask for glo - ry to shine on my name.

I ask for love I can pos - sess.

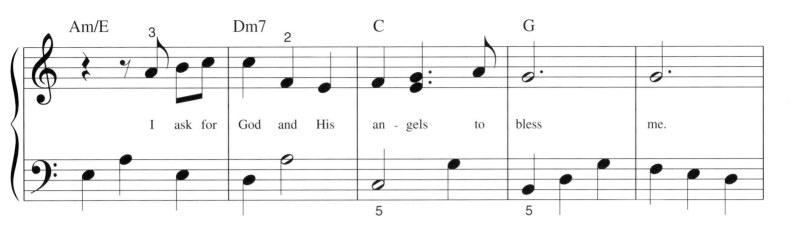

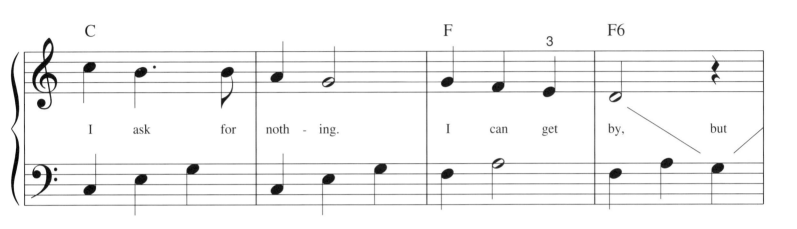

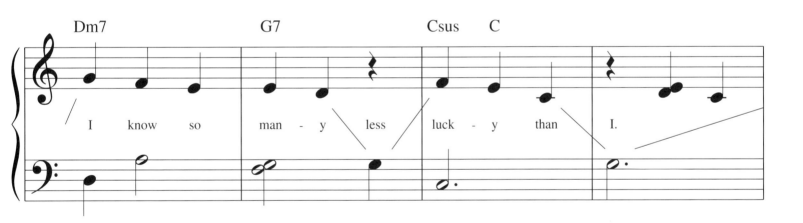

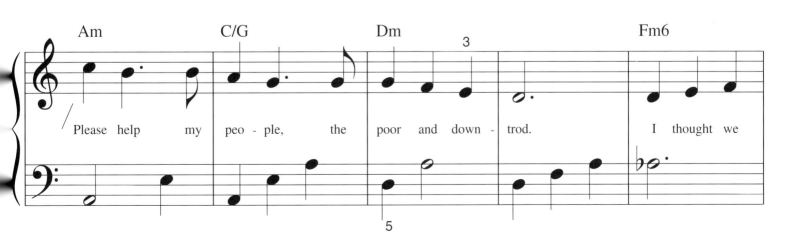

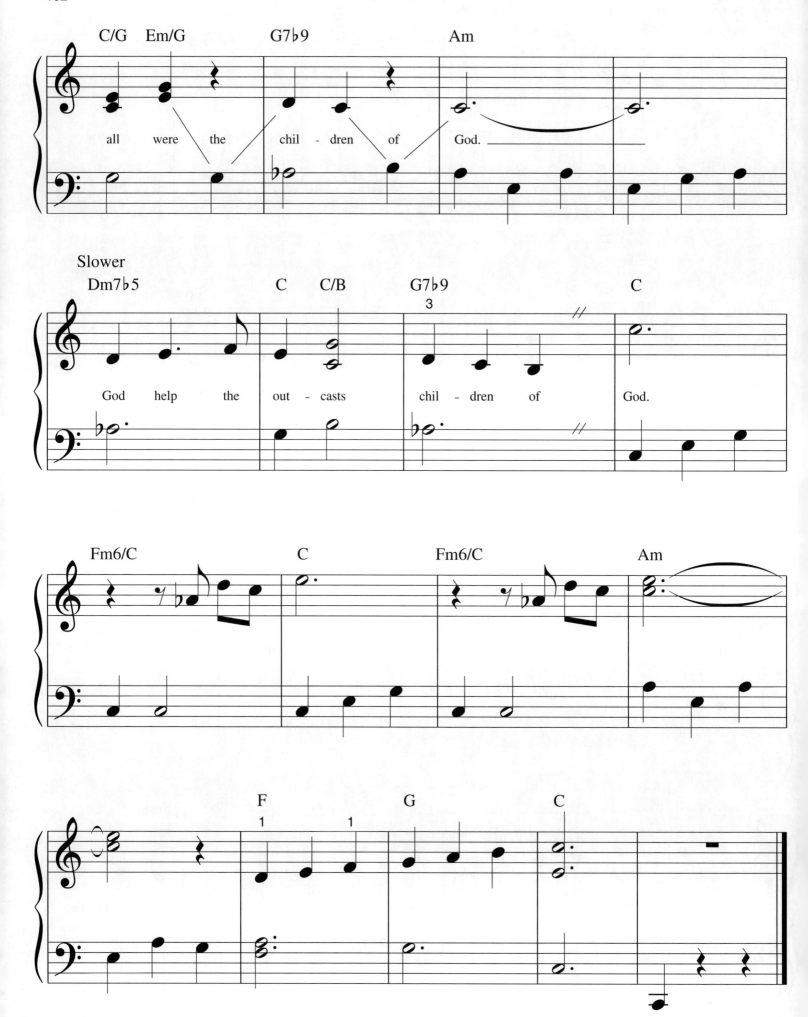

OUT THERE
from Walt Disney's THE HUNCHBACK OF NOTRE DAME

Music by ALAN MENKEN
Lyrics by STEPHEN SCHWARTZ

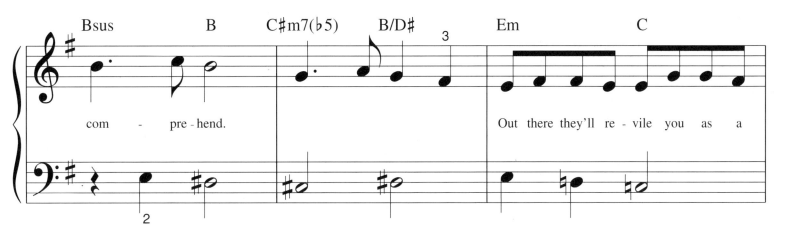

Bsus   B   C#m7(♭5)   B/D#   Em   C

com - pre - hend.   Out there they'll re - vile you as a

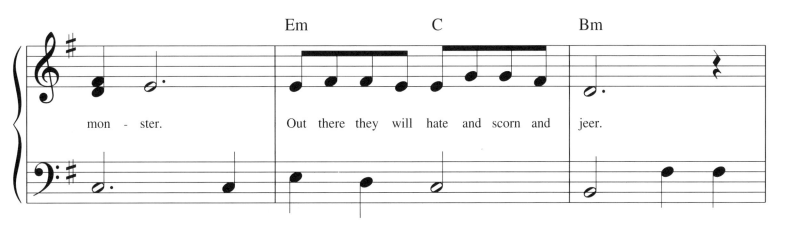

Em   C   Bm

mon - ster.   Out there they will hate and scorn and   jeer.

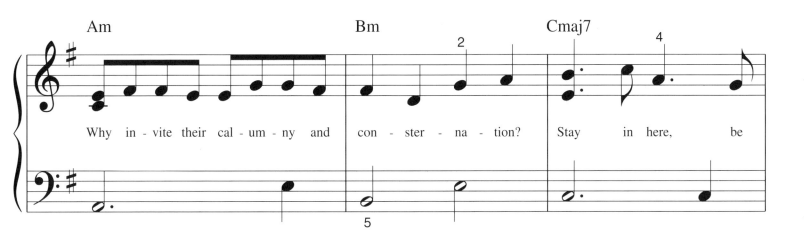

Am   Bm   Cmaj7

Why in - vite their cal - um - ny and   con - ster - na - tion?   Stay in here, be

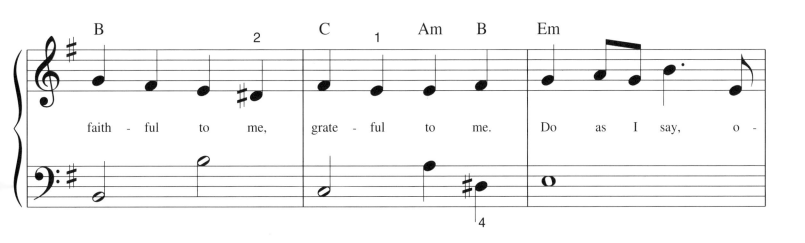

B   C   Am   B   Em

faith - ful to me,   grate - ful to me.   Do as I say, o -

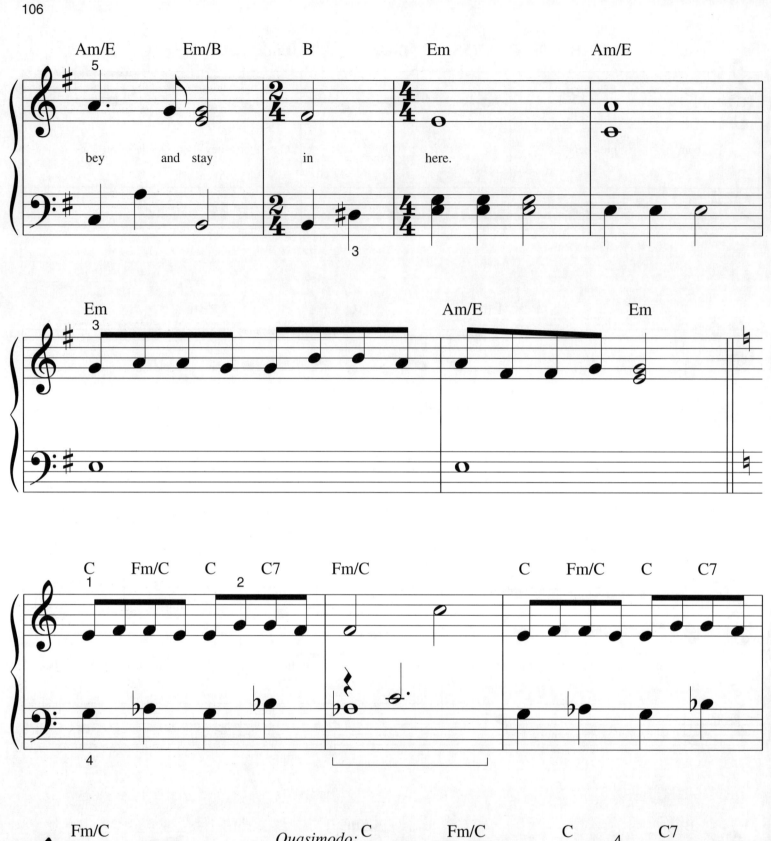

bey   and   stay   in   here.

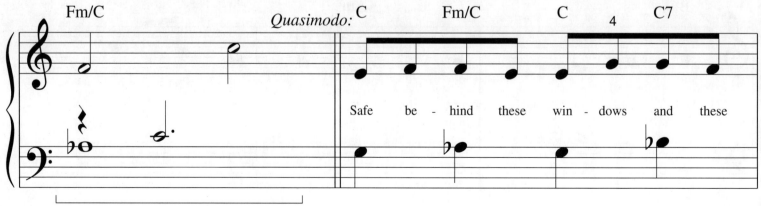

Safe   be - hind   these   win - dows   and   these

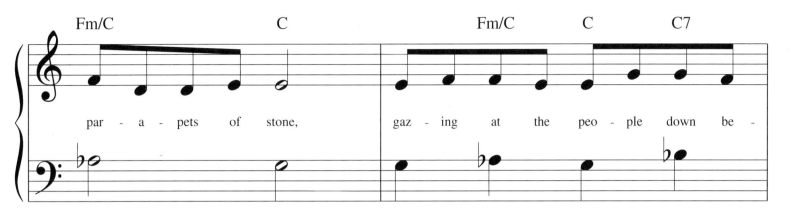

par - a - pets of stone, gaz - ing at the peo - ple down be -

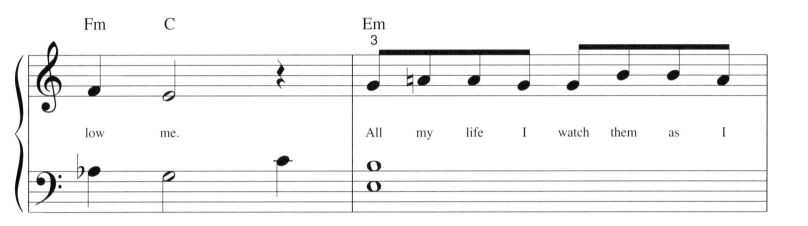

low me. All my life I watch them as I

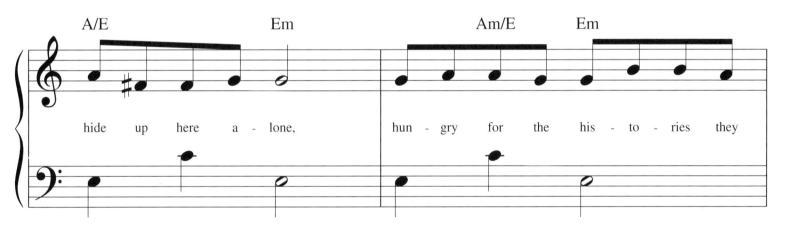

hide up here a - lone, hun - gry for the his - to - ries they

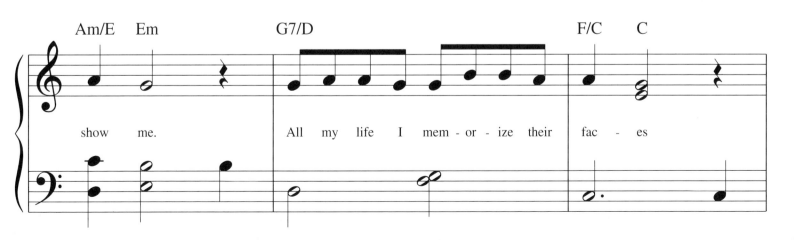

show me. All my life I mem - or - ize their fac - es

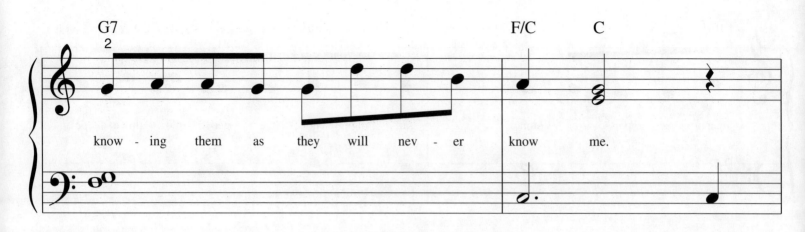

know - ing them as they will nev - er know me.

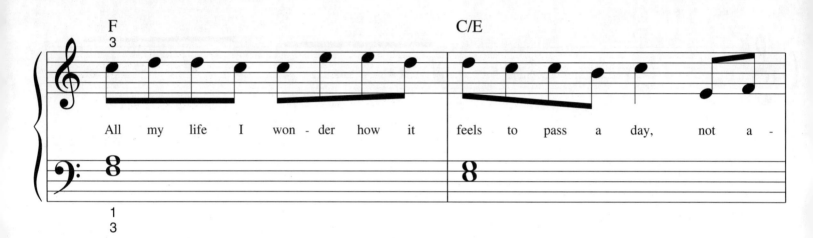

All my life I won - der how it feels to pass a day, not a -

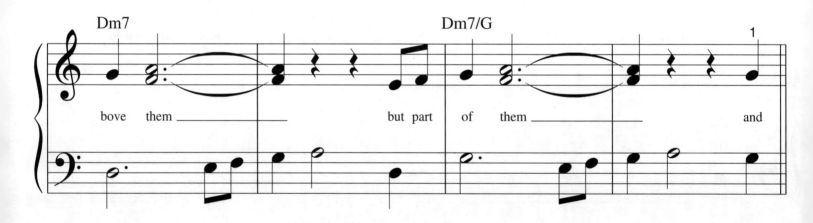

bove them _____ but part of them _____ and

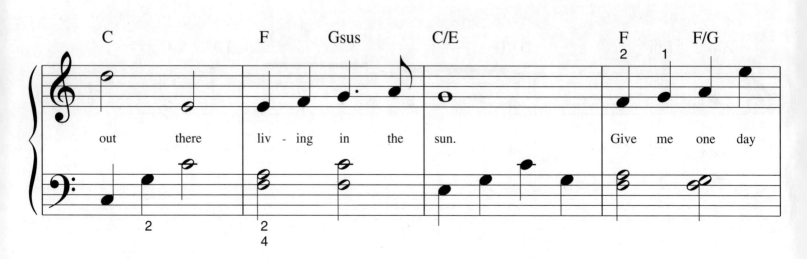

out there liv - ing in the sun. Give me one day

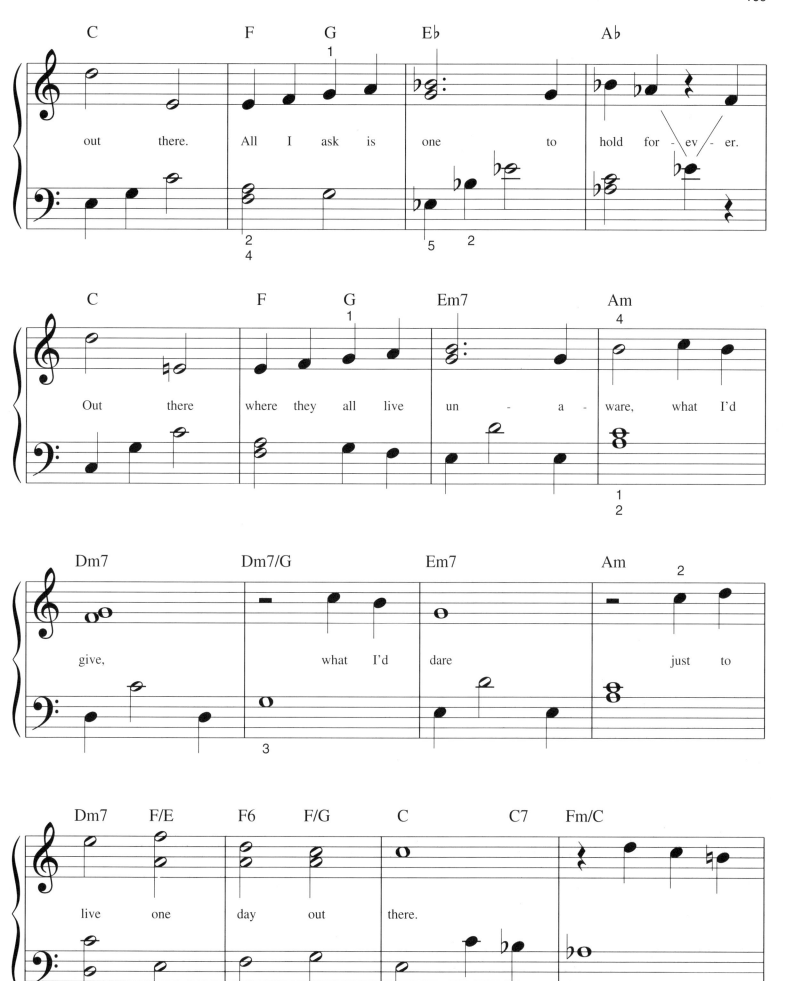

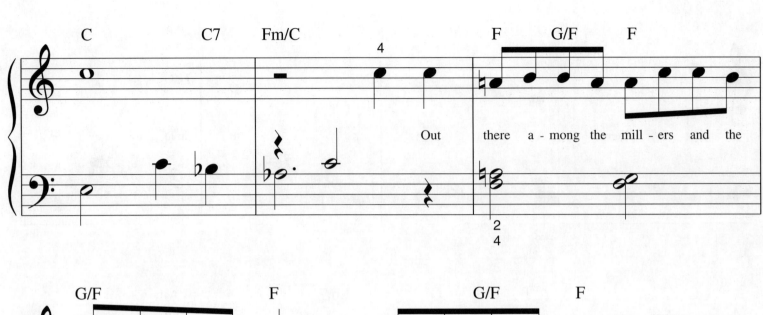

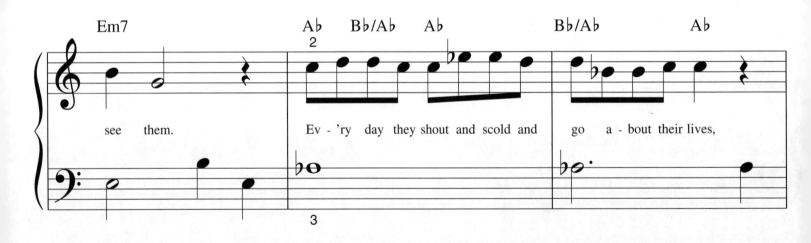

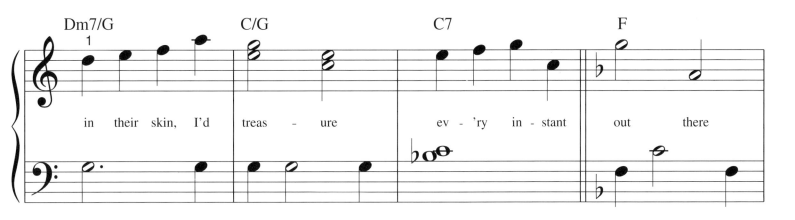

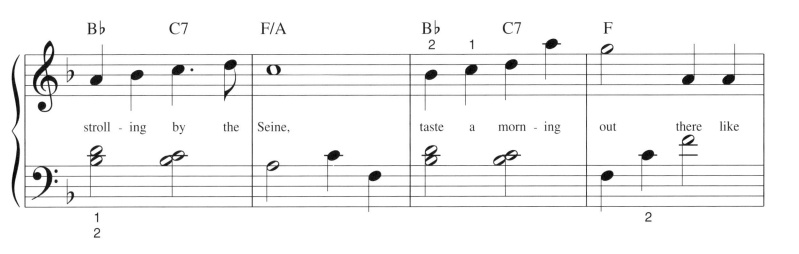

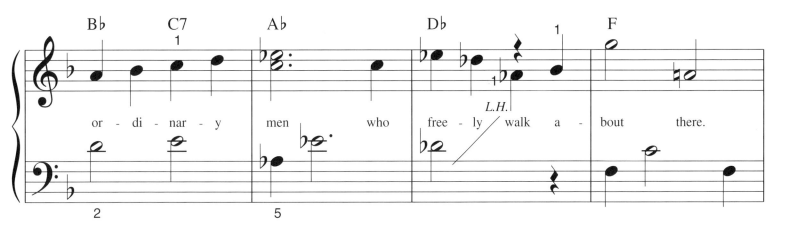

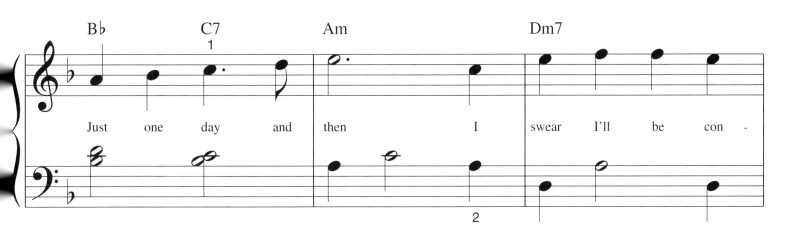

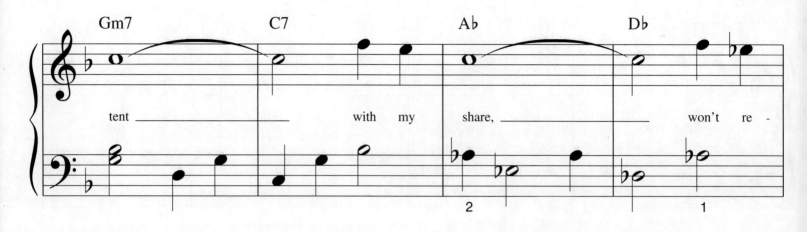

tent _____ with my share, _____ won't re -

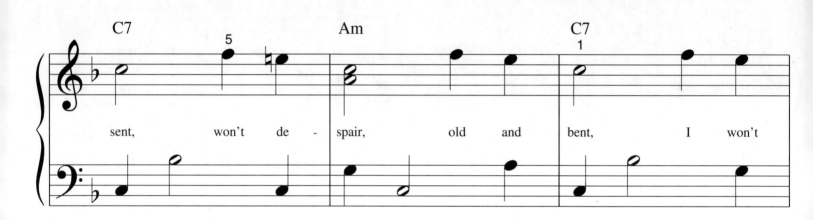

sent, won't de - spair, old and bent, I won't

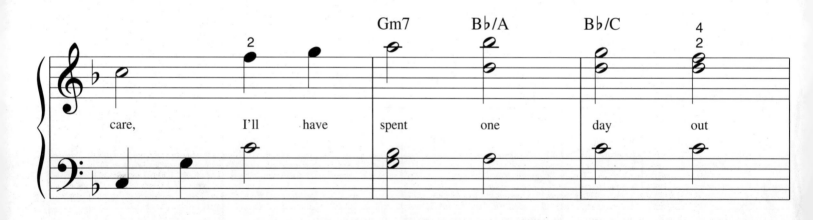

care, I'll have spent one day out

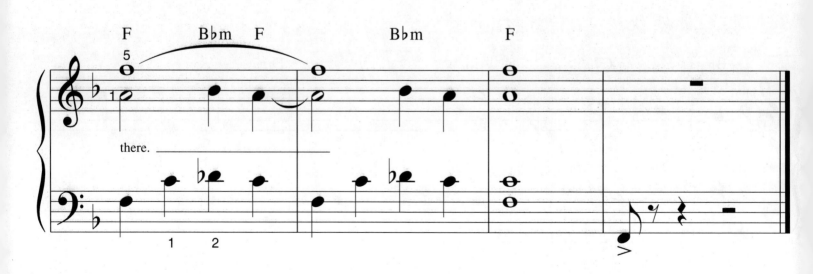

there. _____

SOMEDAY
from Walt Disney's THE HUNCHBACK OF NOTRE DAME

Music by ALAN MENKEN
Lyrics by STEPHEN SCHWARTZ

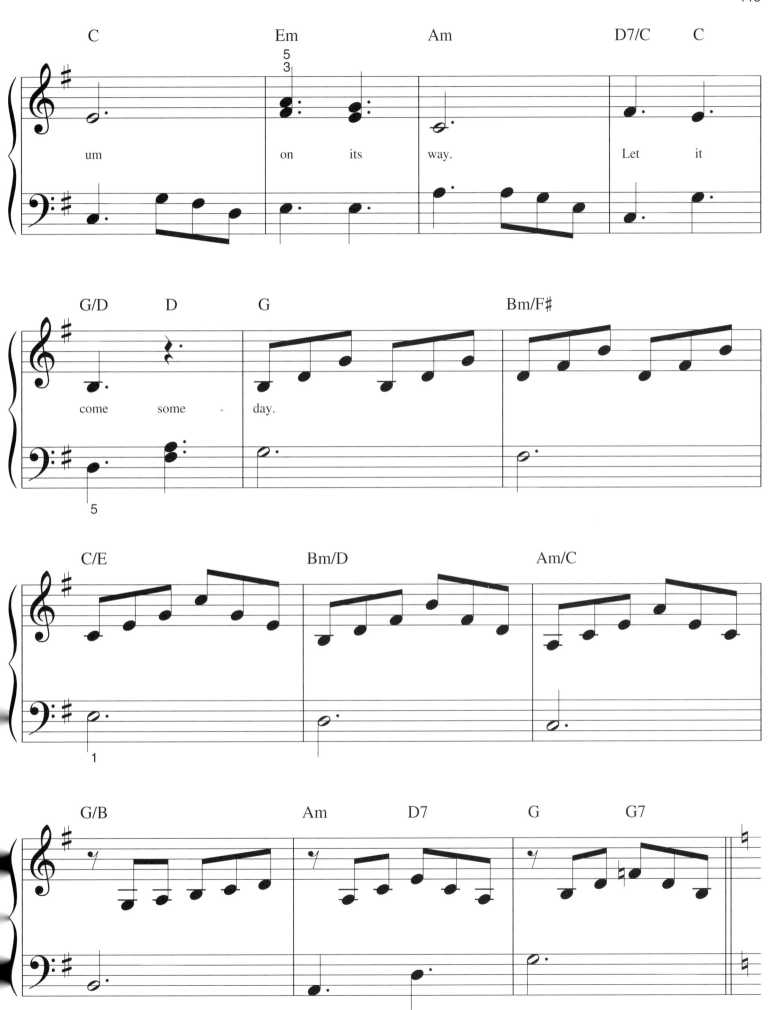

BE PREPARED
from Walt Disney Pictures' THE LION KING

Music by ELTON JOHN
Lyrics by TIM RICE

With a steady beat

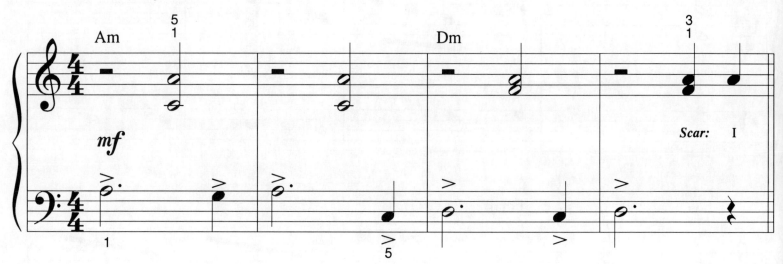

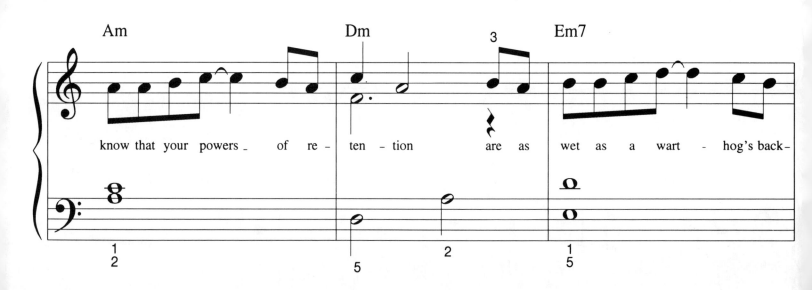

know that your powers _ of re – ten – tion are as wet as a wart – hog's back-

side ___ but thick as you are, ___ pay at – ten -tion: my

120

CAN YOU FEEL THE LOVE TONIGHT

from Walt Disney Pictures' THE LION KING

Music by ELTON JOHN
Lyrics by TIM RICE

CIRCLE OF LIFE
from Walt Disney Pictures' THE LION KING

Music by ELTON JOHN
Lyrics by TIM RICE

all   are   a - greed   as   they | join the stam - pede,   you should
sun   roll - ing   high   through the | sap - phi - re   sky keeps great and

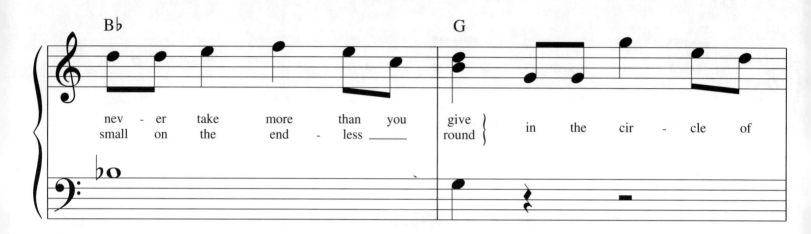

nev - er   take   more   than you | give   in   the   cir - cle of
small   on   the   end - less ____ round

life.   It's the wheel   of | for - tune.

5 2 1 2   1

It's the leap   of | faith.   It's the band of ____

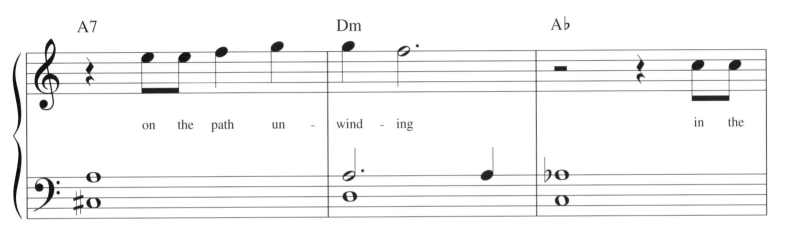

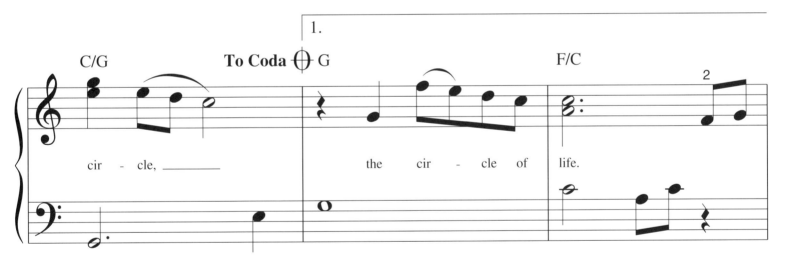

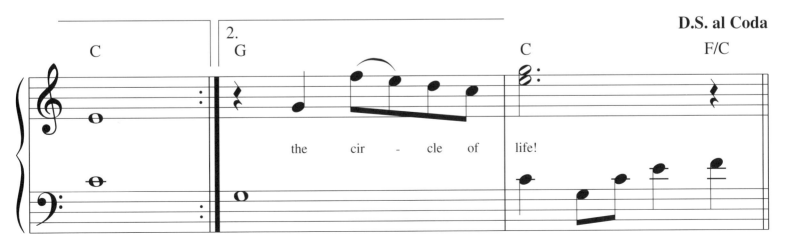

I JUST CAN'T WAIT TO BE KING

from Walt Disney Pictures' THE LION KING

Music by ELTON JOHN
Lyrics by TIM RICE

Happily, with a beat

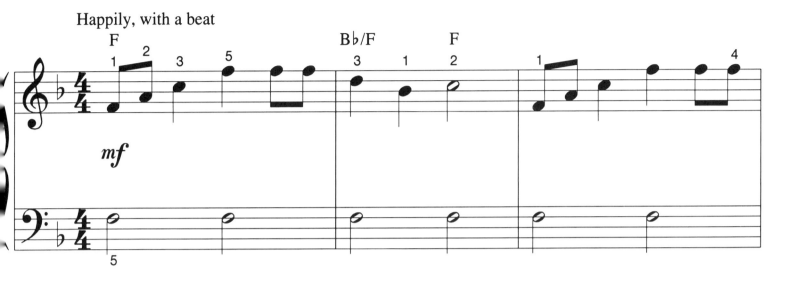

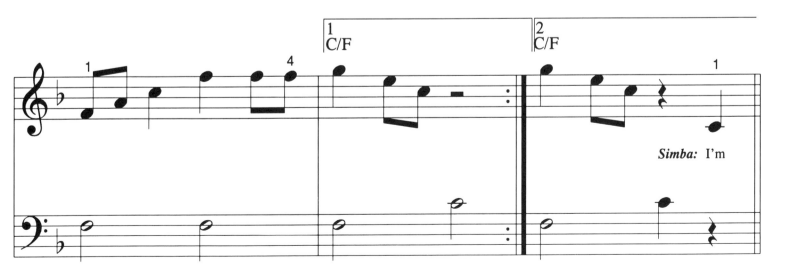

Simba: I'm

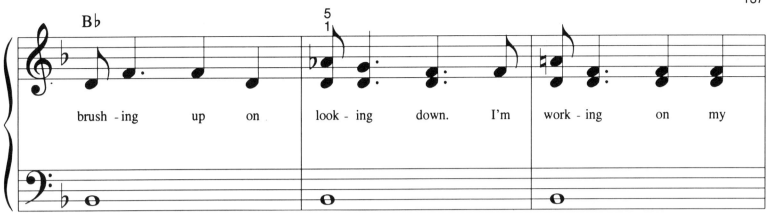

brush - ing up on look - ing down. I'm work - ing on my

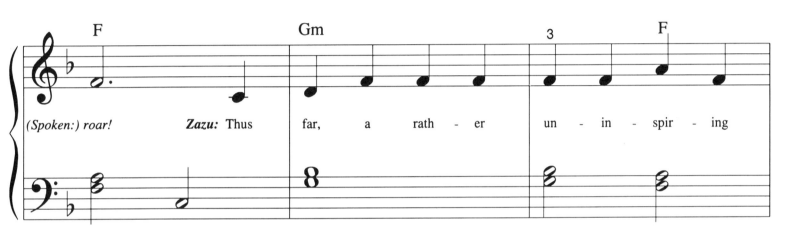

(Spoken:) roar! **Zazu:** Thus far, a rath - er un - in - spir - ing

thing. **Simba:** Oh, I just can't _____

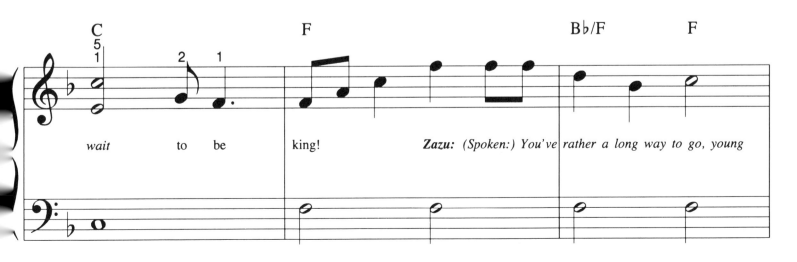

wait to be king! **Zazu:** *(Spoken:) You've rather a long way to go, young*

day,

Well, that's def - i - nite - ly out.

free to do it

all my ____ way!

(Half-spoken:)

Zazu: I think it's time that

you and I ar - ranged a heart to heart.

141

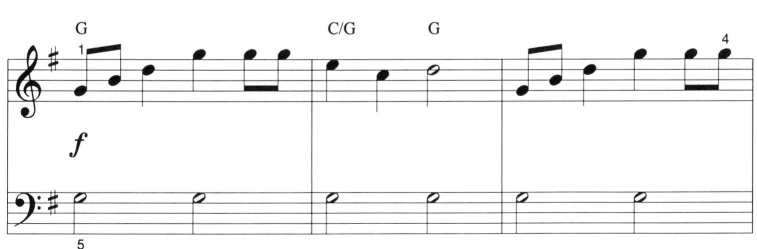

wait to be King. Oh, I just can't ___

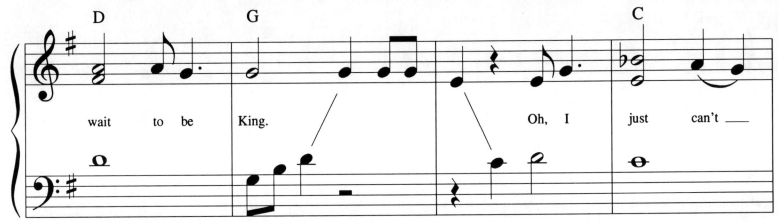

wait to be King. Oh, I just can't ___

wait *mp* *cresc.* *f* to be

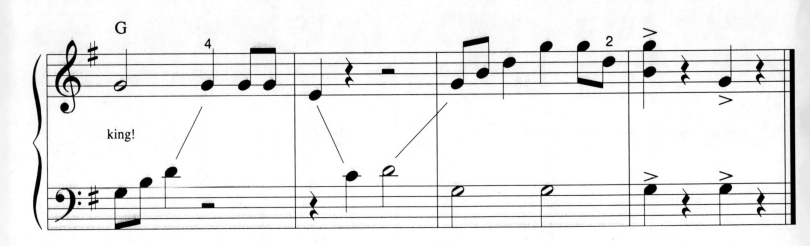

king!

UNDER THE SEA
from Walt Disney's THE LITTLE MERMAID

Lyrics by HOWARD ASHMAN
Music by ALAN MENKEN

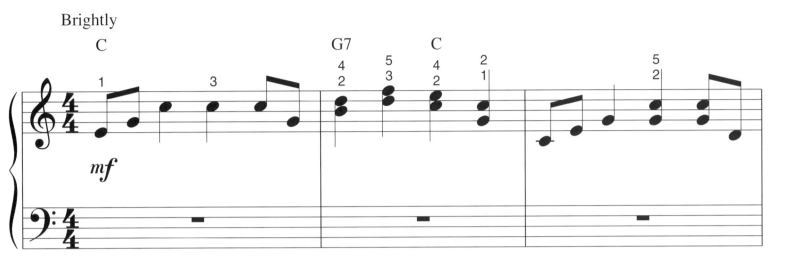

The sea-weed is al - ways green - er
Down here all the fish is hap - py

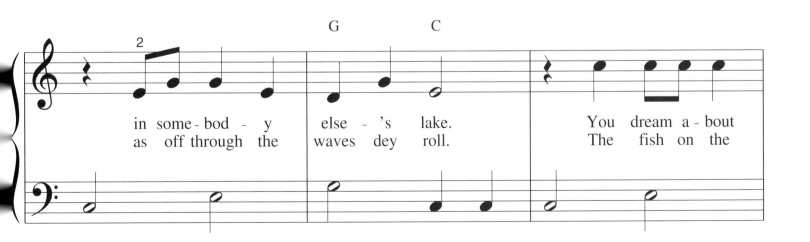

in some-bod - y else - 's lake.
as off through the waves dey roll.

You dream a - bout
The fish on the

146

150

Oh,   that   blow - fish   blow.

Un - der the

154

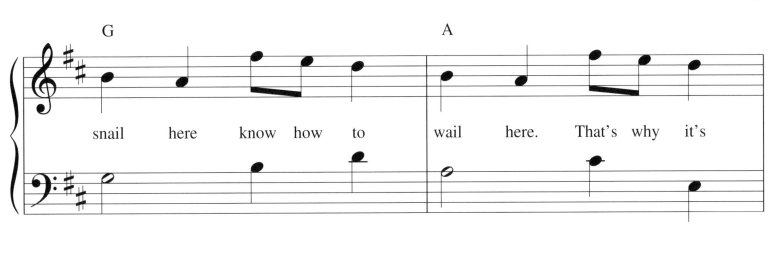

snail here know how to wail here. That's why it's

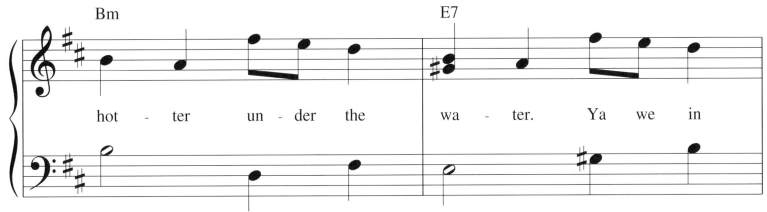

hot - ter un - der the wa - ter. Ya we in

luck here down in the muck here un - der the sea.

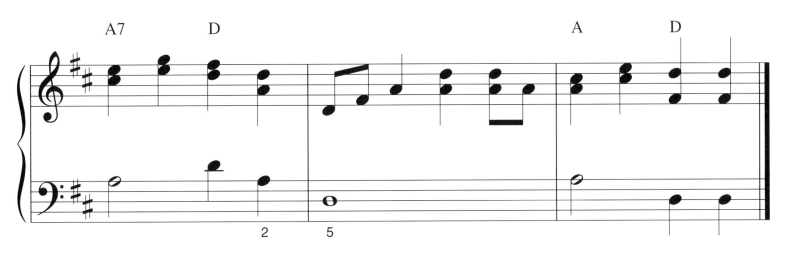

DAUGHTERS OF TRITON
from Walt Disney's THE LITTLE MERMAID

Lyrics by HOWARD ASHMAN
Music by ALAN MENKEN

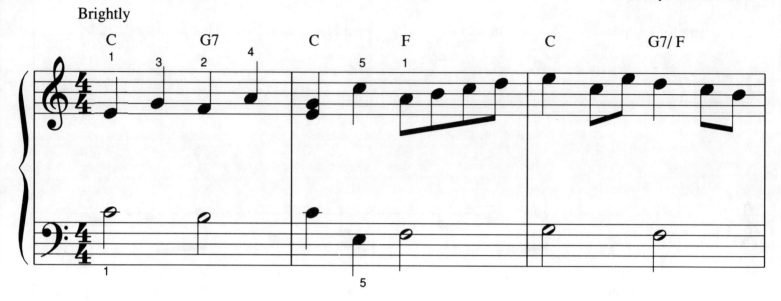

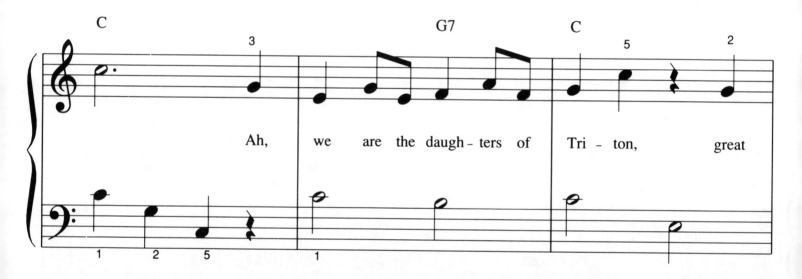

Ah,   we   are the daugh-ters of   Tri-ton,   great

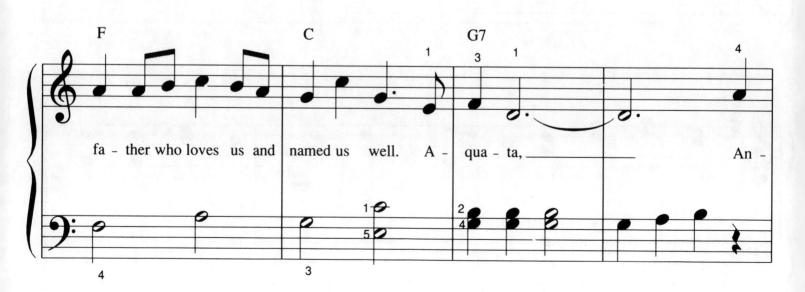

fa-ther who loves us and named us well.   A-qua-ta, _____   An-

LES POISSONS
from Walt Disney's THE LITTLE MERMAID

Lyrics by HOWARD ASHMAN
Music by ALAN MENKEN

Bright Waltz

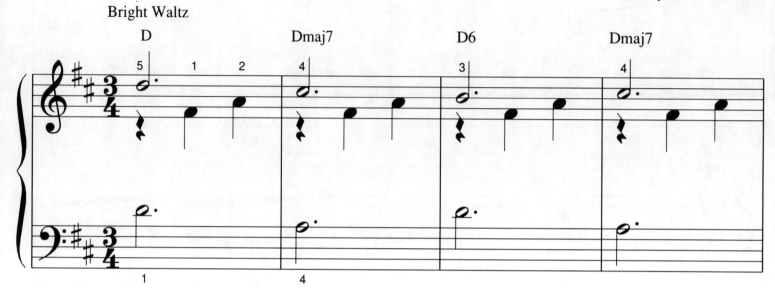

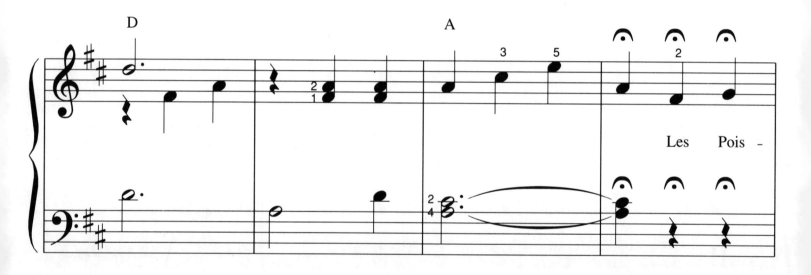

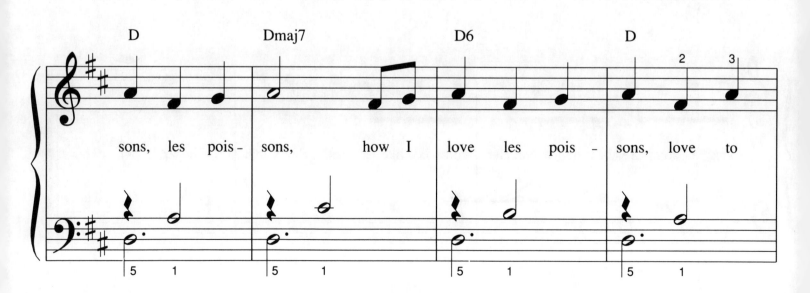

159

162

PART OF YOUR WORLD

from Walt Disney's THE LITTLE MERMAID

Lyrics by HOWARD ASHMAN
Music by ALAN MENKEN

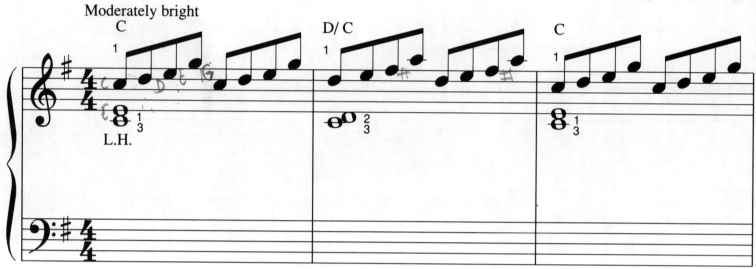

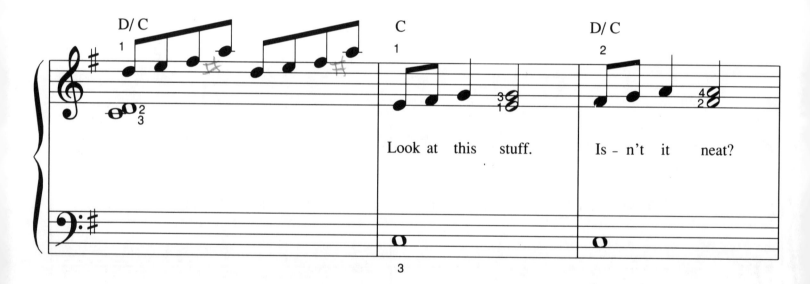

Look at this stuff. Is-n't it neat?

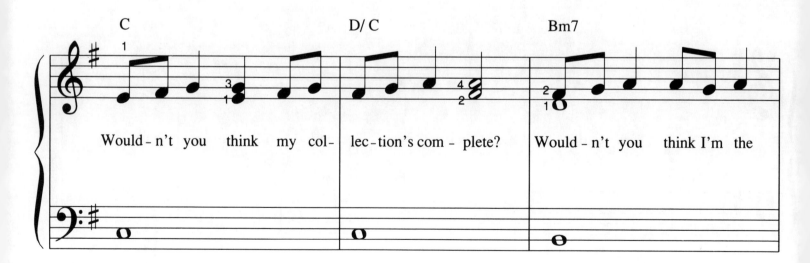

Would-n't you think my col- lec-tion's com- plete? Would-n't you think I'm the

165

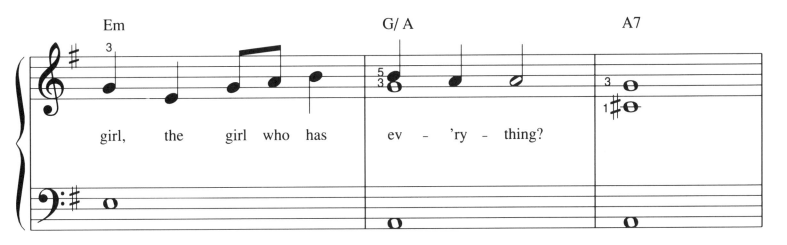

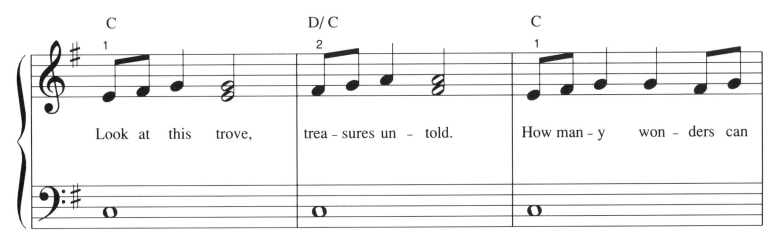

167

Cm

bove,

out of the the sea.

slower

G

D

Wish I could be part of that world.

C

L.H.

a tempo

D/ C

C

D/ C

G

HONOR TO US ALL
from Walt Disney Pictures' MULAN

Music by MATTHEW WILDER
Lyrics by DAVID ZIPPEL

Bather: This is what you give me to work with. Well, hon-ey, I've seen worse. We're going to turn this sow's ear in-to a silk purse.

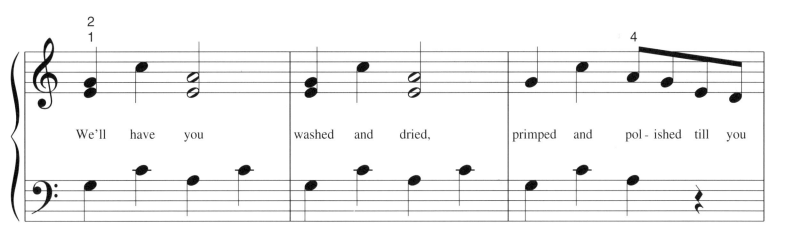

We'll have you washed and dried, primped and pol - ished till you

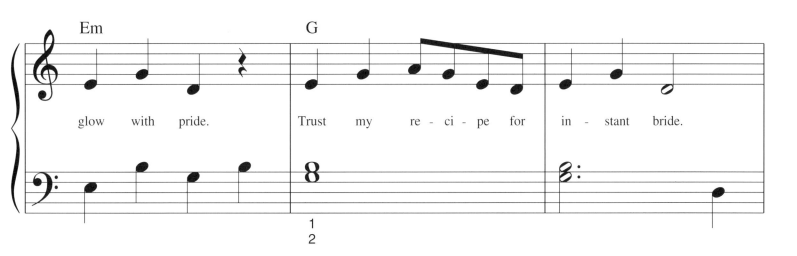

glow with pride. Trust my re - ci - pe for in - stant bride.

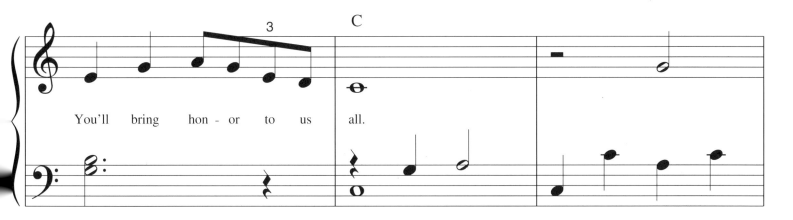

You'll bring hon - or to us all.

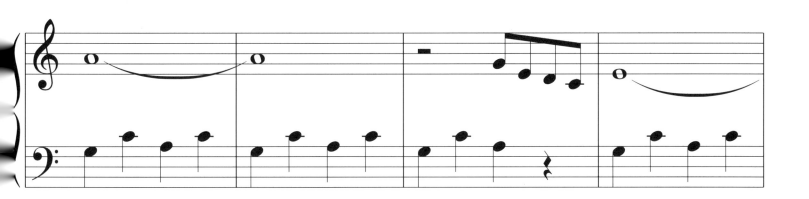

Hairdresser 1:
Wait and see. When we're through

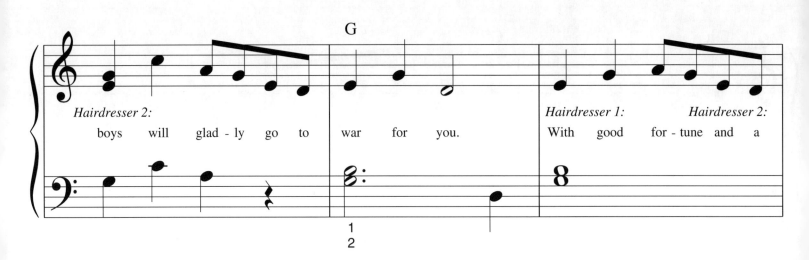

G

Hairdresser 2:
boys will glad - ly go to war for you.

Hairdresser 1: *Hairdresser 2:*
With good for - tune and a

1
2

C

great hair - do

Hairdressers 1, 2 & Fa Li:
you'll bring hon - or to us all.

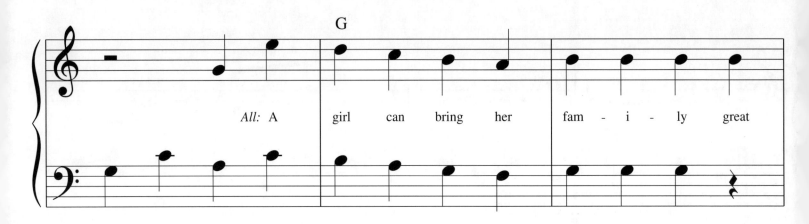

G

All: A girl can bring her fam - i - ly great

you can't fail, like a lo-tus blos-som, soft and pale.

How could an-y fel-low say "No sale"? You'll bring hon-or to us

all.

Add pedal

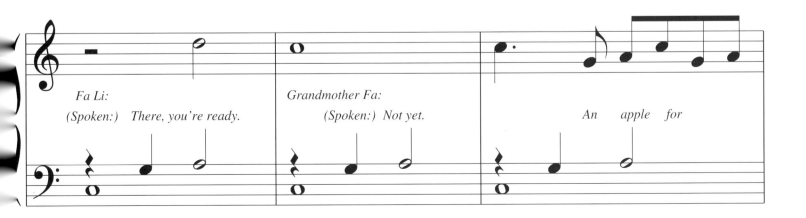

Fa Li:
(Spoken:) There, you're ready.

Grandmother Fa:
(Spoken:) Not yet.

An apple for

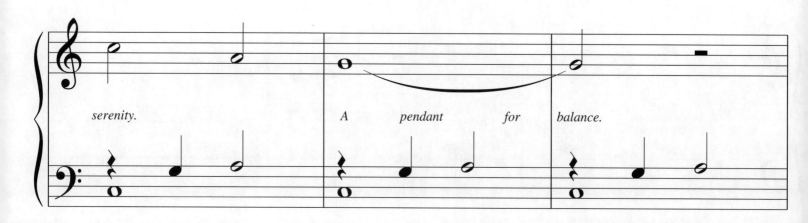

serenity. *A* *pendant* *for* *balance.*

(Sung:) Beads of jade for beau - ty.

Am

You must proud - ly show it.

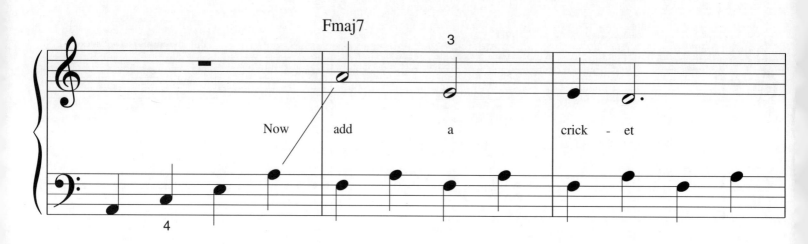

Fmaj7

Now add a crick - et

just for luck and e - ven you can't

G

No pedal

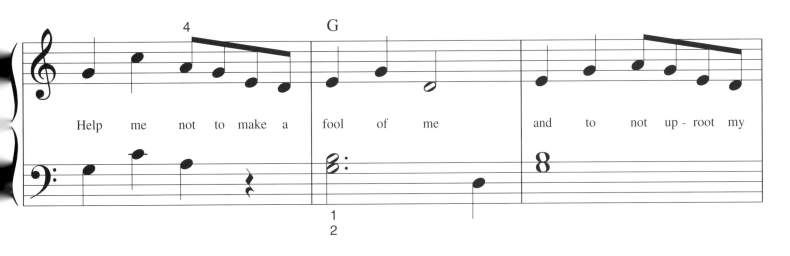

blow it.

C

Mulan:
An - ces - tors, hear my plea.

Help me not to make a fool of me and to not up-root my

G

fam - 'ly tree. Keep my fa - ther stand - ing tall.

Am7   Am/G

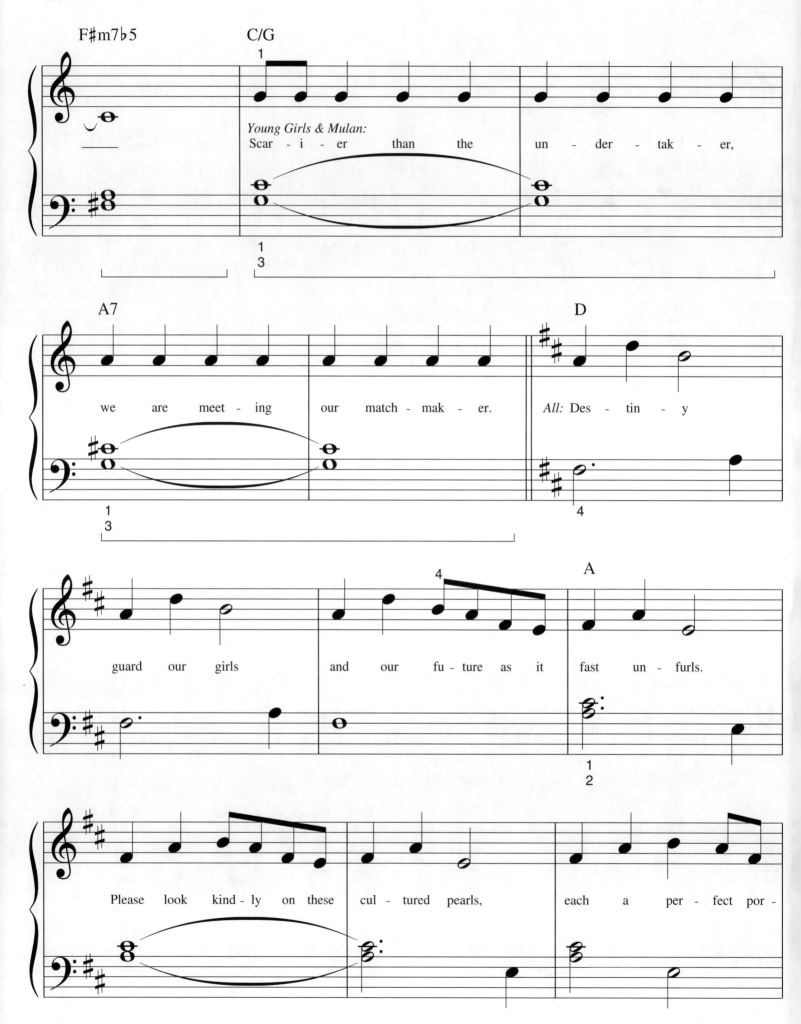

REFLECTION
from Walt Disney Pictures' MULAN

Music by MATTHEW WILDER
Lyrics by DAVID ZIPPEL

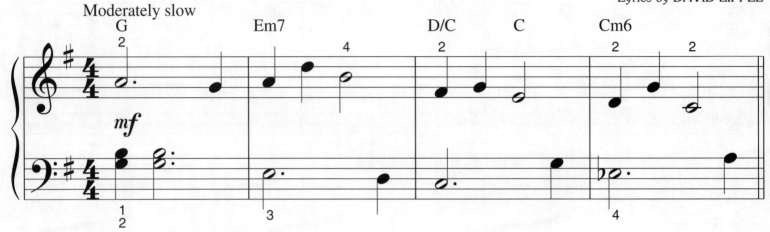

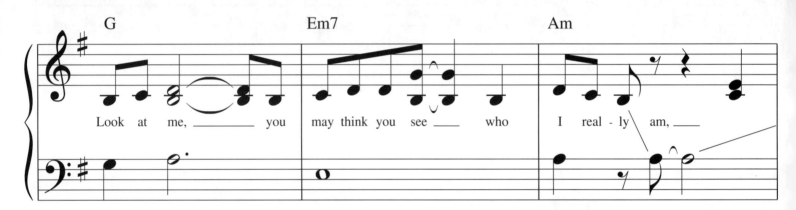

Look at me, _____ you may think you see _____ who I real-ly am, _____

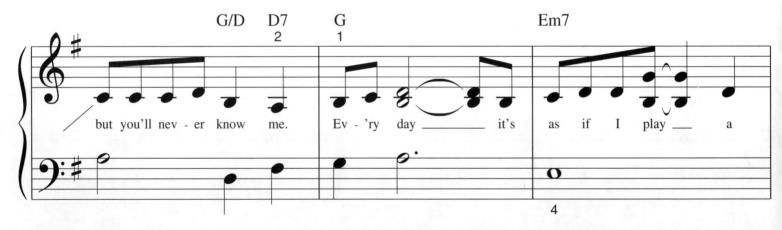

but you'll nev-er know me. Ev-'ry day _____ it's as if I play _____ a

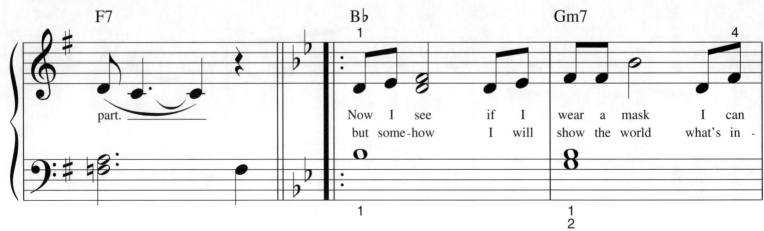

part. _____

Now I see if I wear a mask I can
but some-how I will show the world what's in-

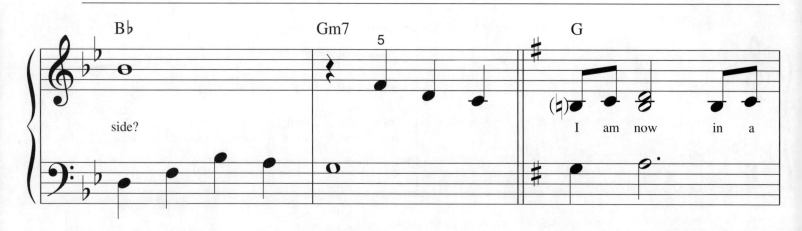

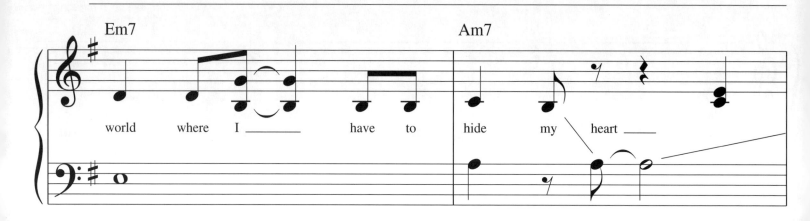

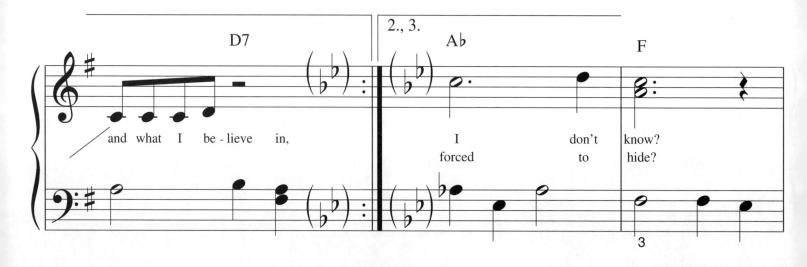

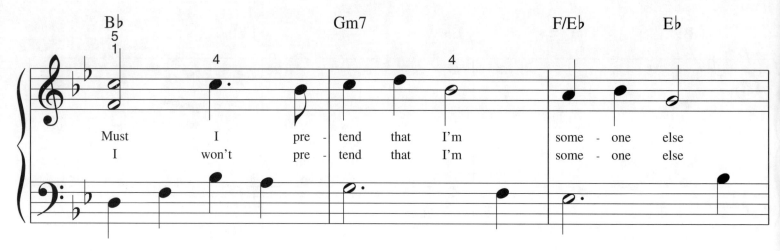

185

TRUE TO YOUR HEART

from Walt Disney Pictures' MULAN

Music by MATTHEW WILDER
Lyrics by DAVID ZIPPEL

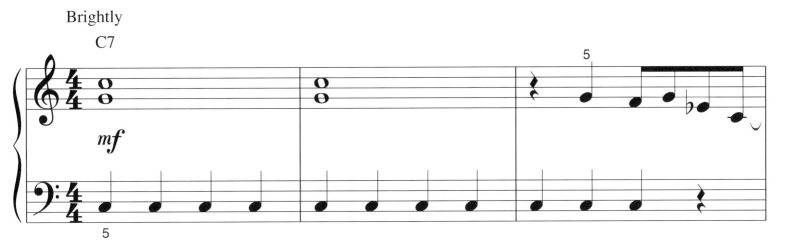

Ba - by, I knew at once that you were meant for me.

Deep in my soul, I know that I'm your des - ti - ny. Though

F7   G7

you're un - sure,   why fight the tide? Don't think so much,   let your

                                    C7

heart de - cide. _____   Ba - by, I see your fu - ture, and it's
                              Some-one you know is on your side can

true to your heart. That's when the heav-ens will part, and ba - by,

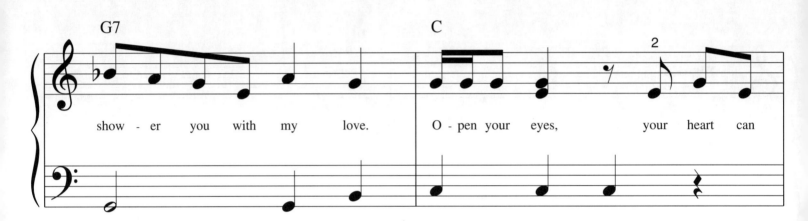

show - er you with my love. O - pen your eyes, your heart can

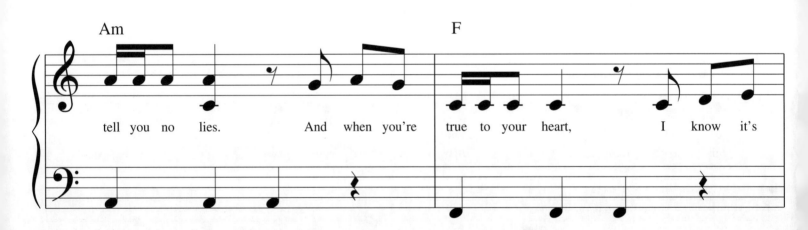

tell you no lies. And when you're true to your heart, I know it's

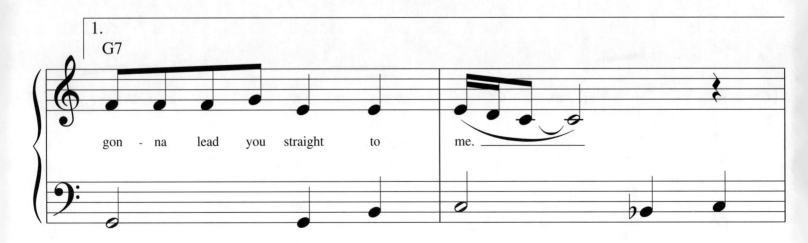

1.

gon - na lead you straight to me.

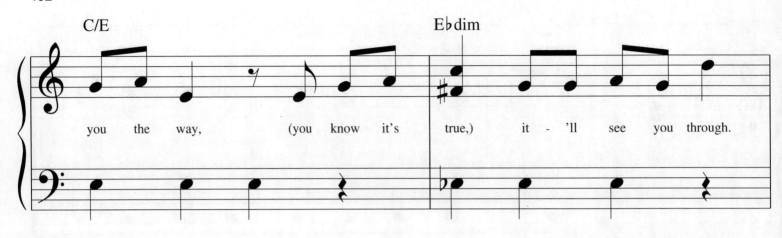

you the way, (you know it's true,) it-'ll see you through.

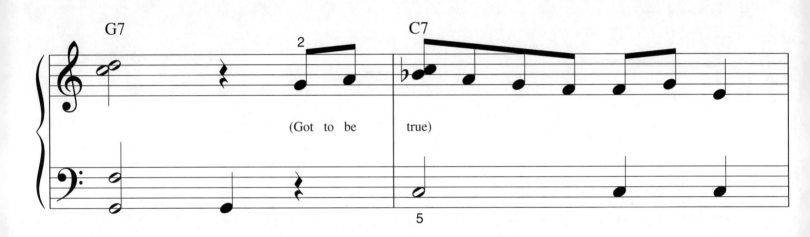

(Got to be true)

(to your heart.)

Girl, my heart is driv-ing me to where you are;

you can take both hands off the wheel and still get far. Be _____

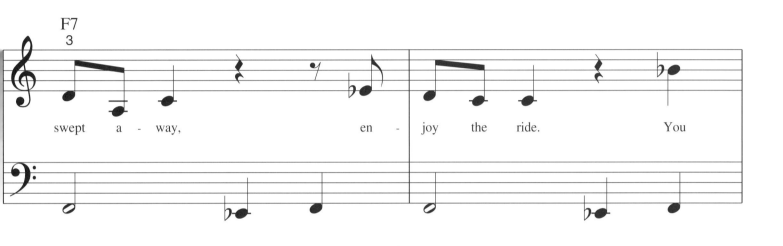

F7

swept a - way, en - joy the ride. You

G7

won't get lost with your heart to ____ guide you.

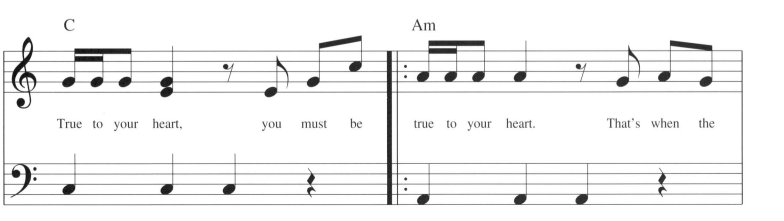

C

True to your heart, you must be

Am

true to your heart. That's when the

heav - ens will part, and ba - by, show - er you with my love.

O - pen your eyes, your heart can tell you no lies. And when you're

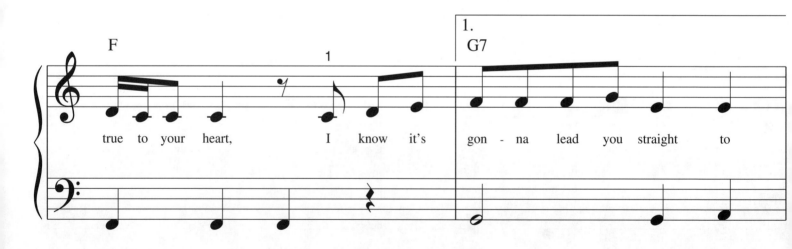

true to your heart, I know it's gon - na lead you straight to

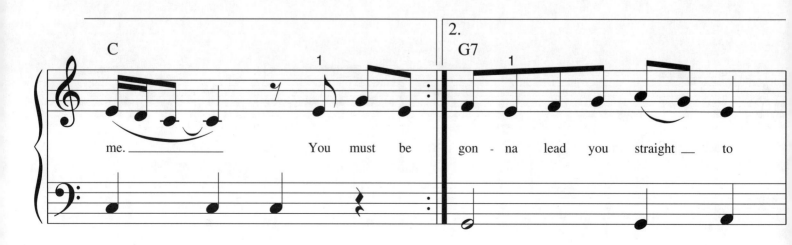

me. _____ You must be gon - na lead you straight __ to

C7

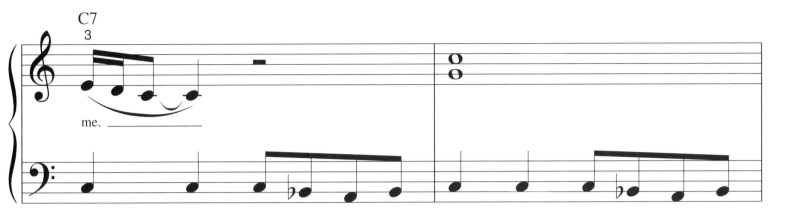

me. _____

C7

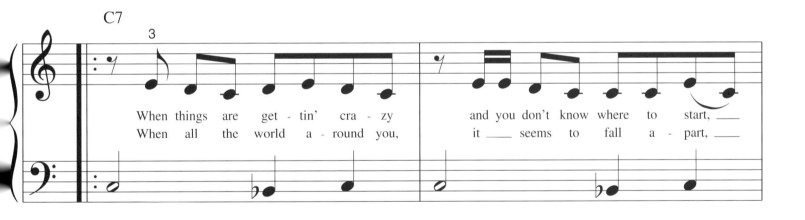

When things are get - tin' cra - zy and you don't know where to start, ____
When all the world a - round you, it ____ seems to fall a - part, ____

keep on be - liev - ing, ba - by; just be true to your heart.
keep on be - liev - ing, ba - by; just be true to your heart.

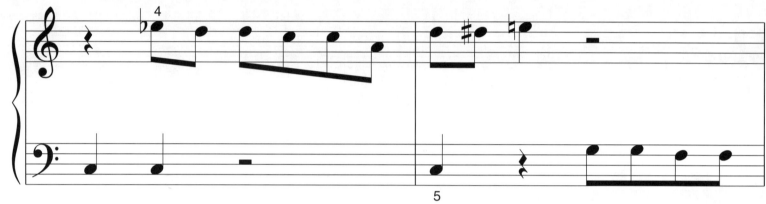

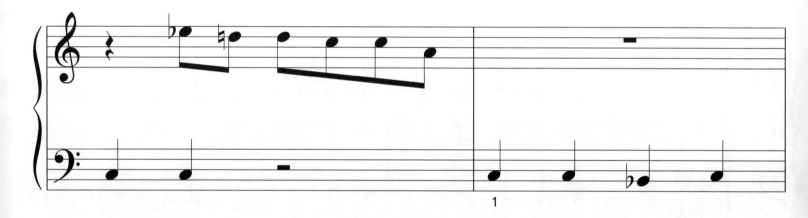

Repeat and Fade

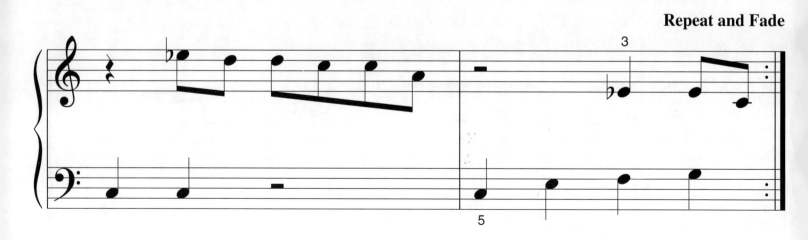

COLORS OF THE WIND

from Walt Disney's POCAHONTAS

Music by ALAN MENKEN
Lyrics by STEPHEN SCHWARTZ

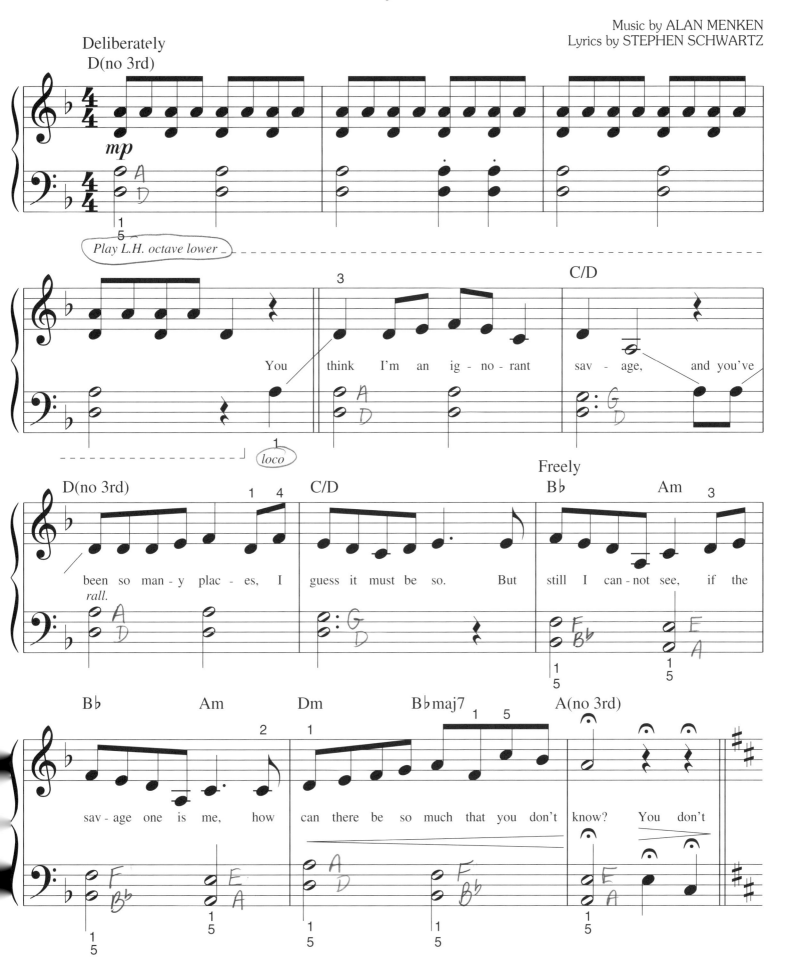

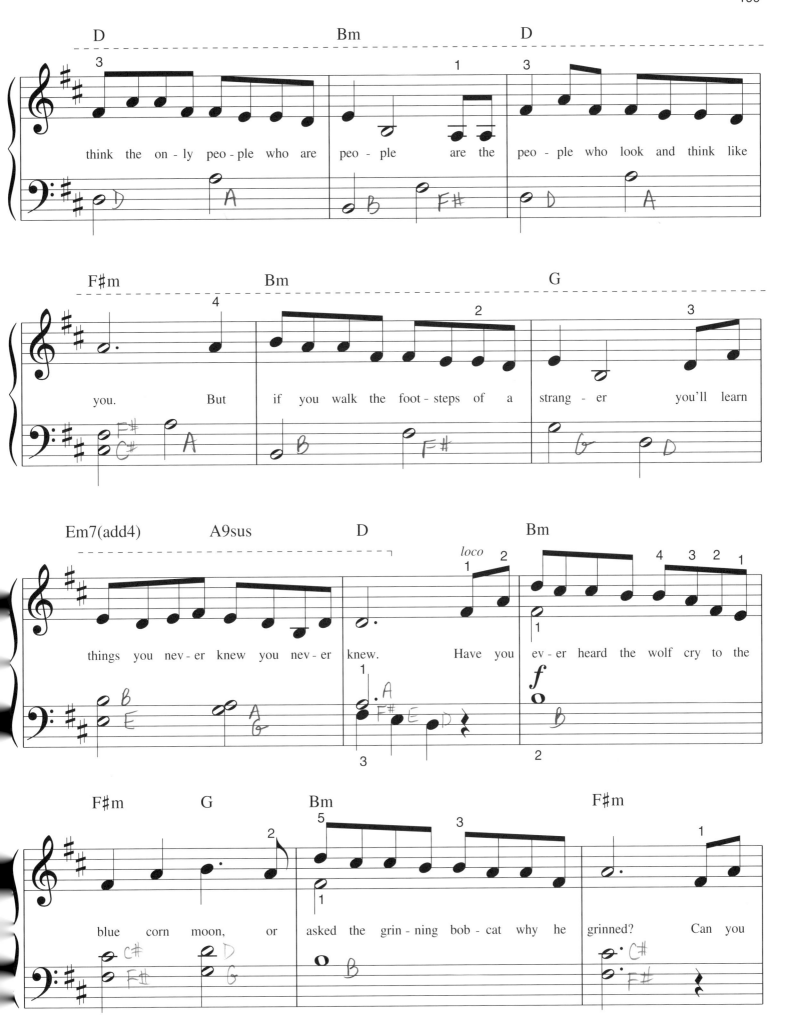

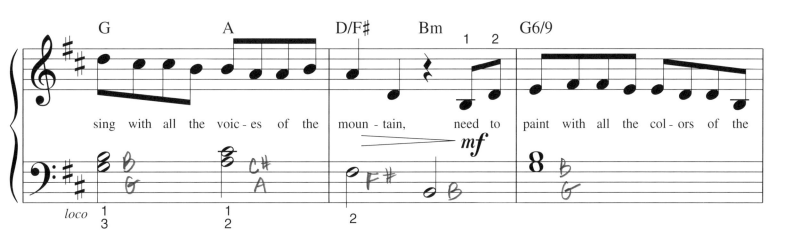

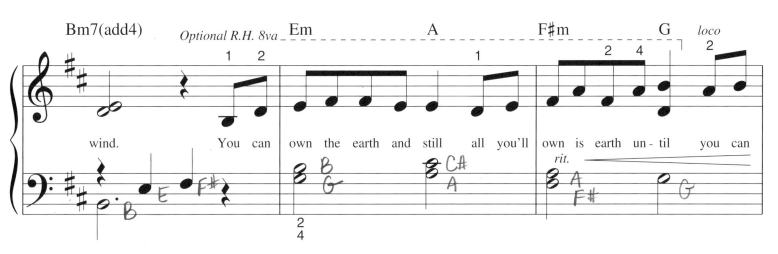

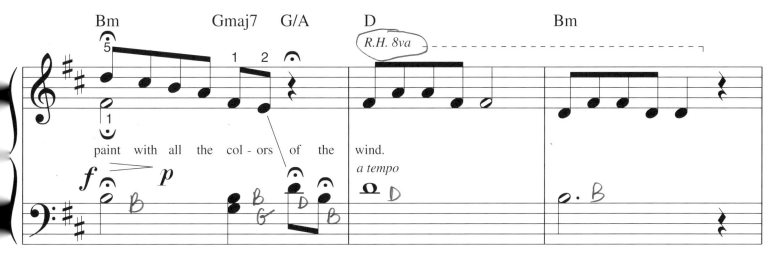

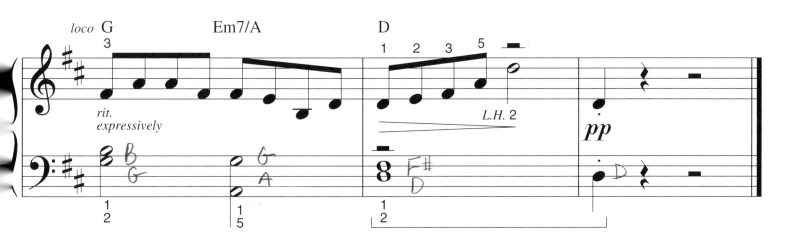

IF I NEVER KNEW YOU

(Love Theme from POCAHONTAS)
from Walt Disney's POCAHONTAS

Music by ALAN MENKEN
Lyrics by STEPHEN SCHWARTZ

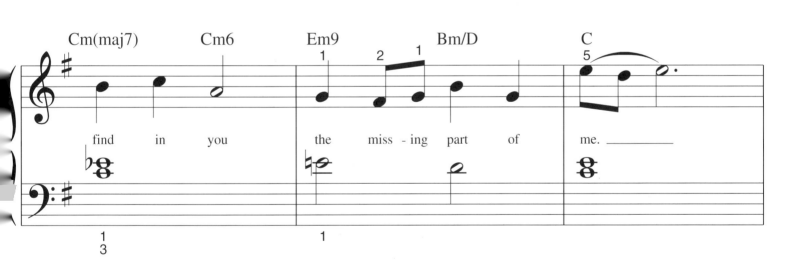

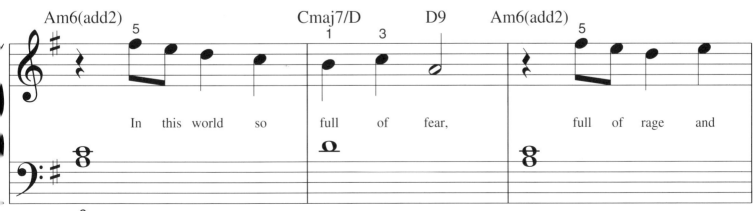

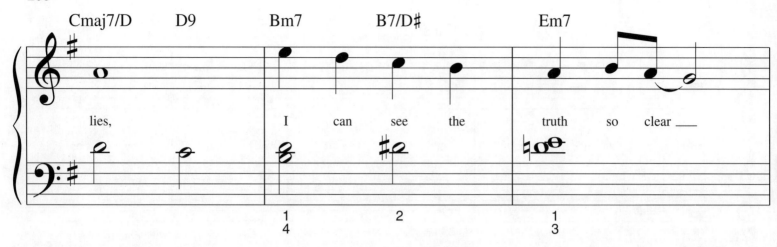

Cmaj7/D   D9   Bm7   B7/D#   Em7

lies,   I   can   see   the   truth   so   clear

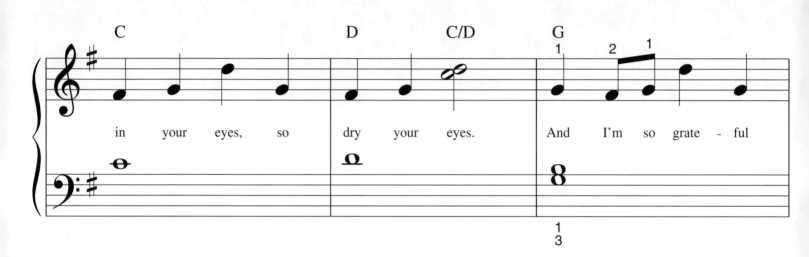

C   D   C/D   G

in   your   eyes,   so   dry   your   eyes.   And   I'm   so   grate - ful

Em   G   C

to   you.   I'd   have   lived   my   whole   life   through,

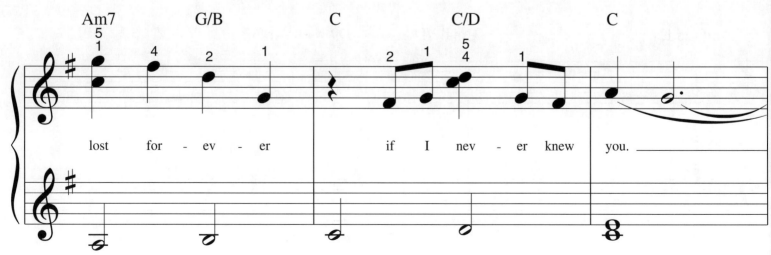

Am7   G/B   C   C/D   C

lost   for - ev - er   if   I   nev - er   knew   you.

C   C/D   D/C   C

if I nev - er knew *Male:* you. I thought our love would be so

D/C   C   D/C   Bm7

beau - ti - ful. *Female:* Some - how we'd make the whole world

D/E

bright. _____ *Both:* I nev - er knew that fear and

Cmaj7   G/B   Em   Bm7

hate could be so strong, all they'd leave us were these whis - pers in the

night, _____ But still my heart is say - ing we were

right. _____ *Female:* Oh. _____ If I nev - er

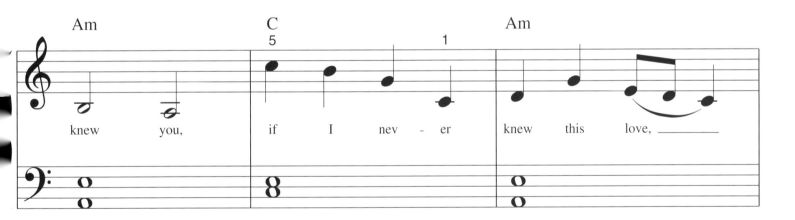

knew you, if I nev - er knew this love, _____

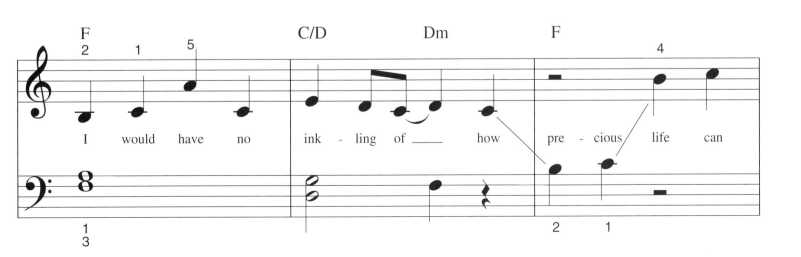

I would have no ink - ling of ____ how pre - cious life can

F/G   G   F/G   Em/G   F/G   G

be. _____

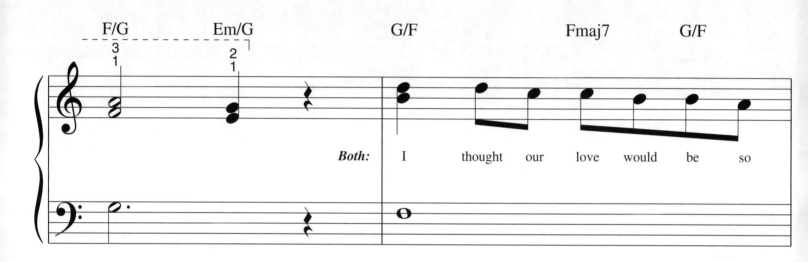

F/G   Em/G   G/F   Fmaj7   G/F

Both: I   thought   our   love   would   be   so

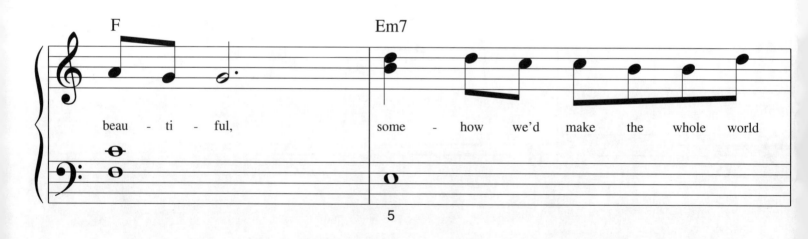

F   Em7

beau - ti - ful,   some - how we'd make the whole world

5

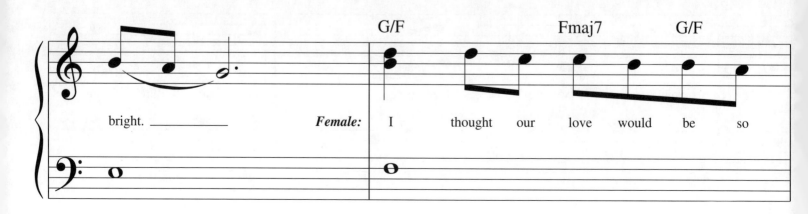

G/F   Fmaj7   G/F

bright. _____   **Female:** I   thought   our   love   would   be   so

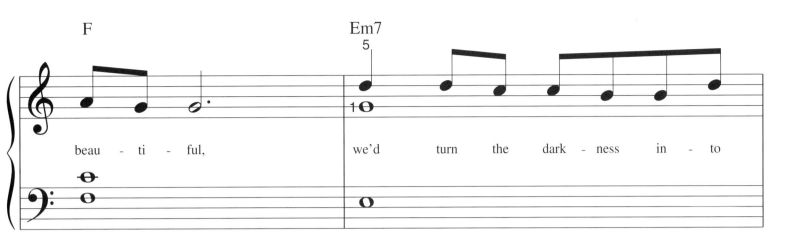

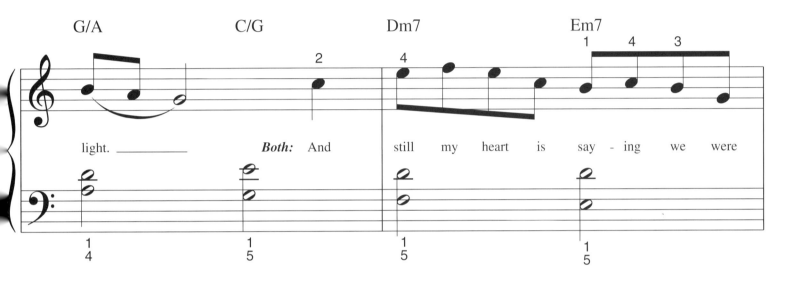

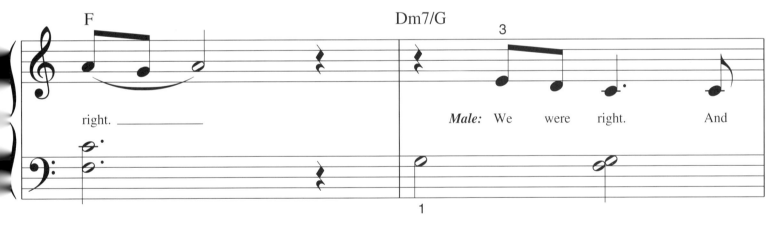

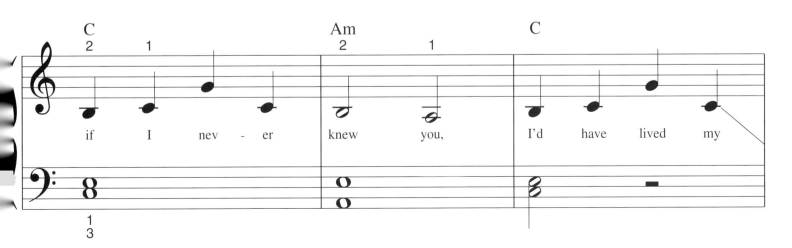

JUST AROUND THE RIVERBEND

from Walt Disney's POCAHONTAS

Music by ALAN MENKEN
Lyrics by STEPHEN SCHWARTZ

With motion

flow - ing. But peo - ple, I guess, can't live like that; we

all must pay a price: to be safe we lose our chance of ev - er

know - ing what's a - round the riv - er - bend,

wait - ing just a - round the riv - er - bend.

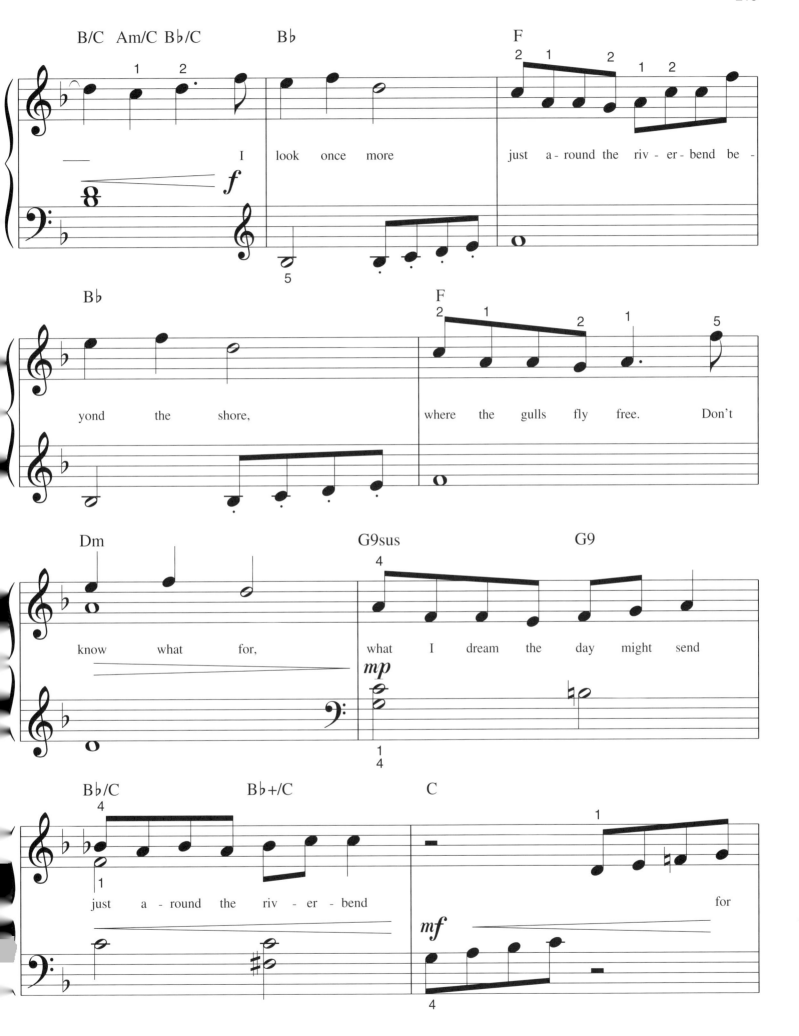

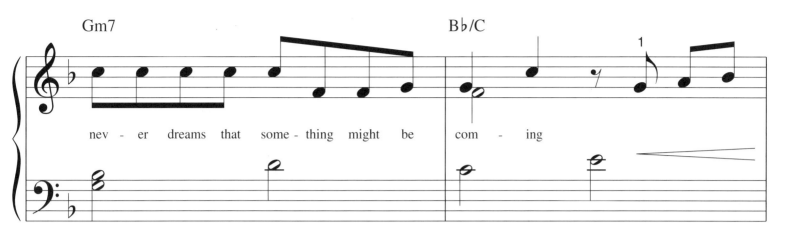

never dreams that some-thing might be com-ing

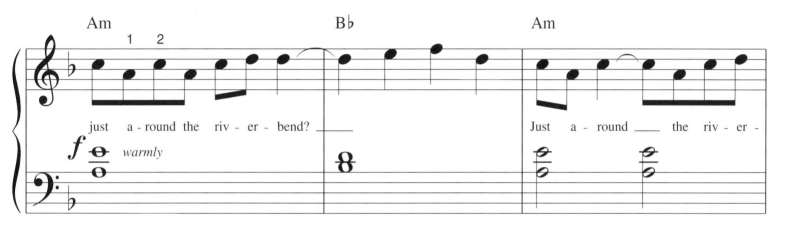

just a-round the riv-er-bend? ____ Just a-round ____ the riv-er-

bend. I look once more just a-round the riv-er-bend be-

yond the shore, some-where past the sea. Don't know what for...

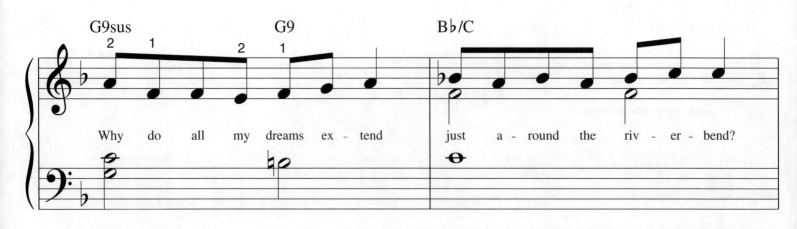

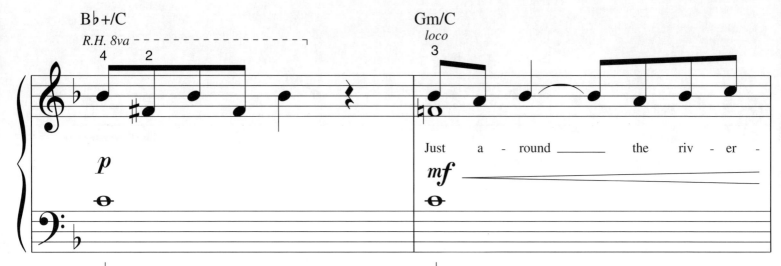

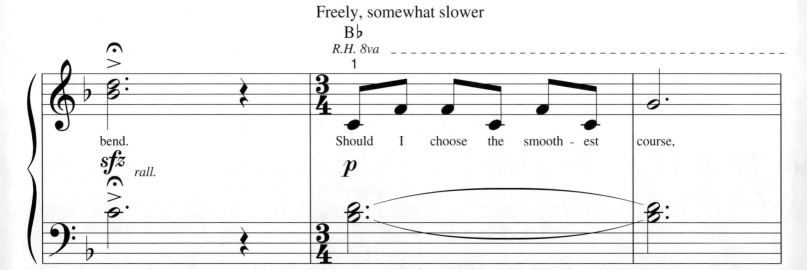

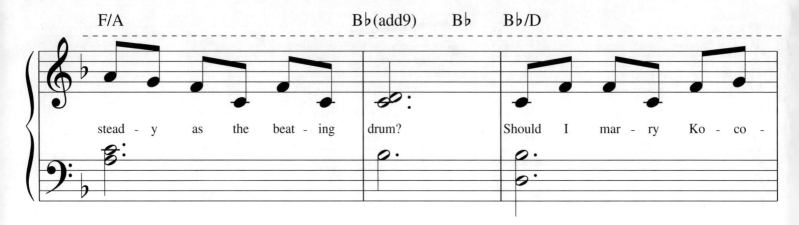

LISTEN WITH YOUR HEART

from Walt Disney's POCAHONTAS

Music by ALAN MENKEN
Lyrics by STEPHEN SCHWARTZ

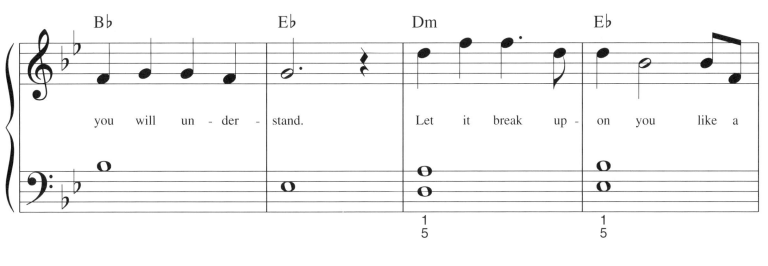

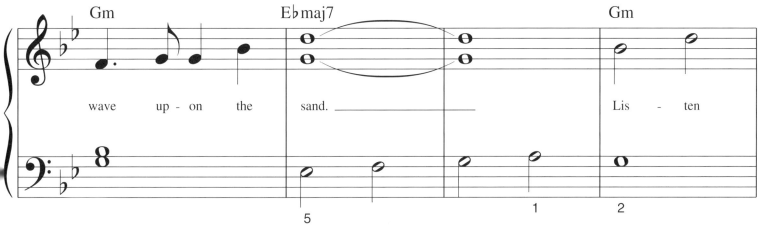

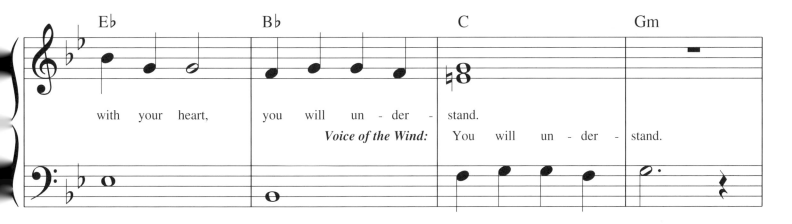

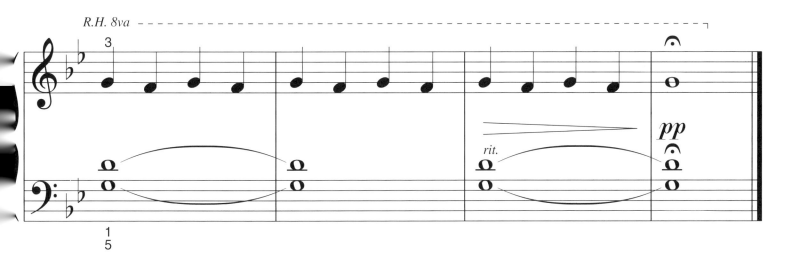

STRANGERS LIKE ME

from Walt Disney Pictures' TARZAN™

Words and Music by
PHIL COLLINS

Fast, with a steady beat

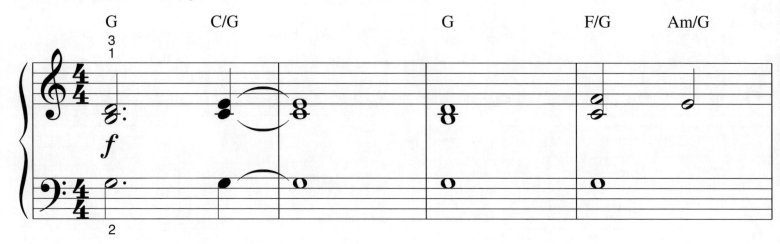

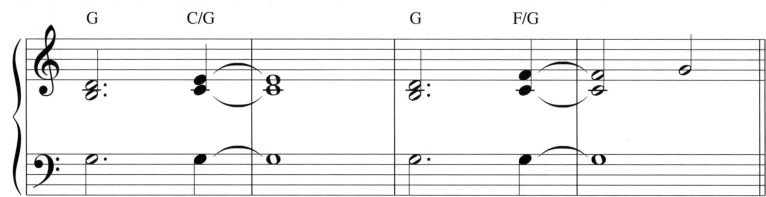

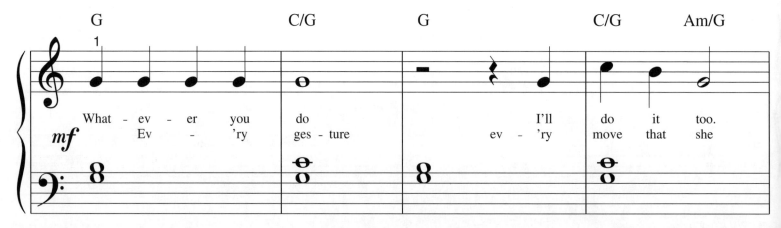

Whatever you do I'll do it too.
Ev - 'ry ges - ture ev - 'ry move that she

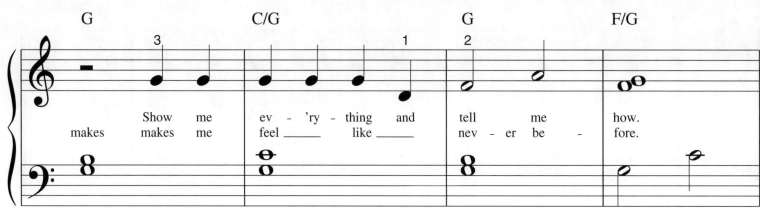

Show me ev - 'ry - thing and tell me how.
makes makes me feel _____ like _____ nev - er be - fore.

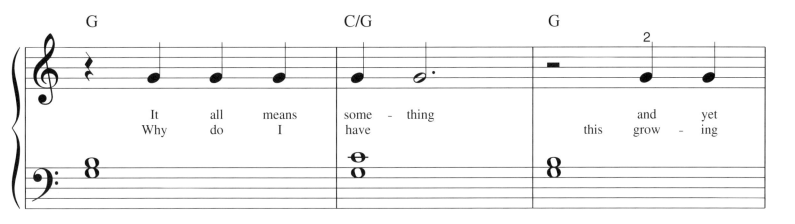

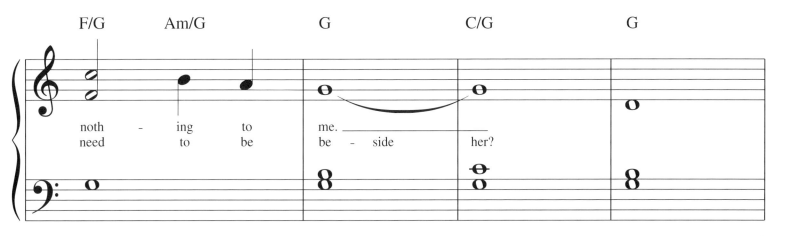

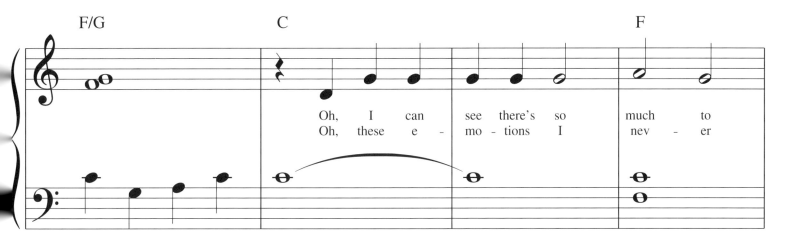

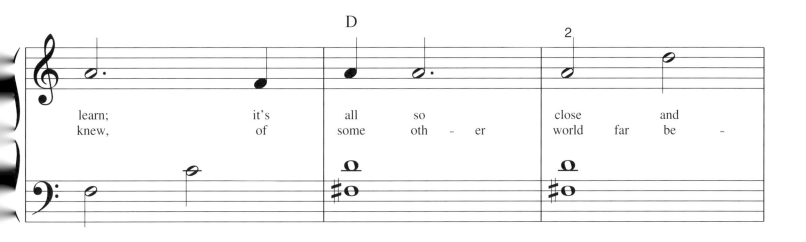

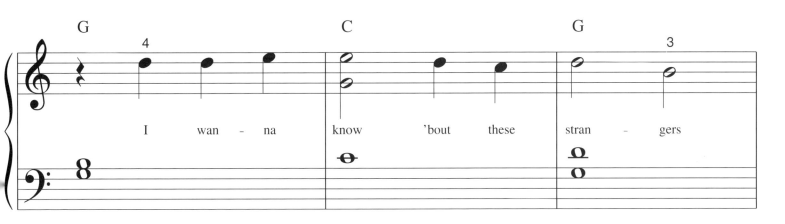

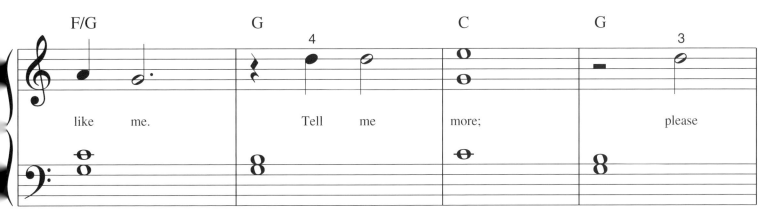

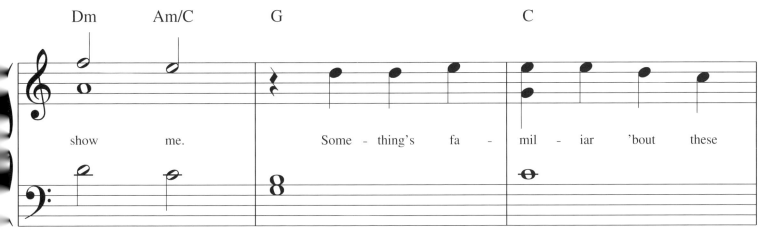

To Coda

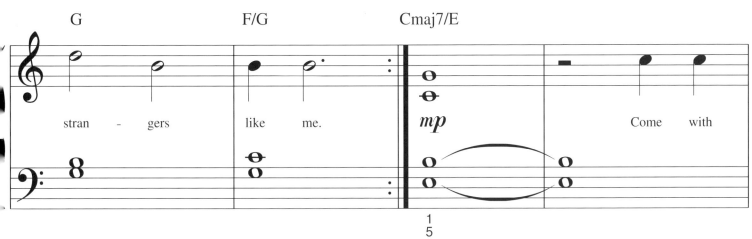

With pedal

226

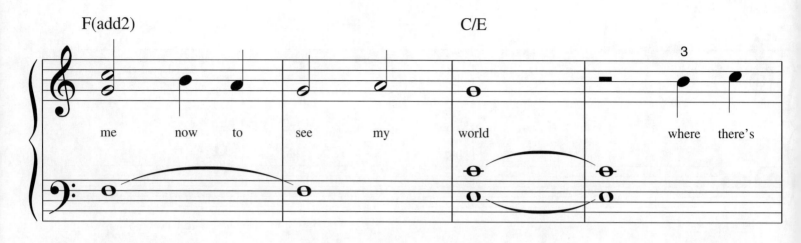

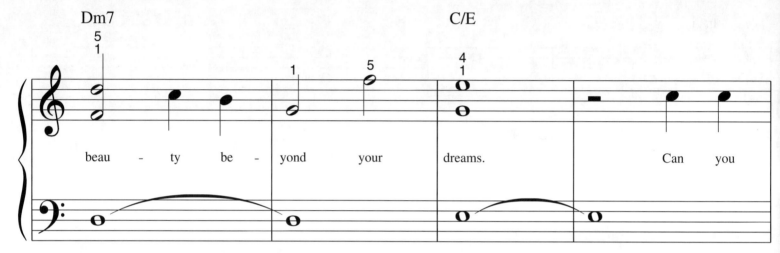

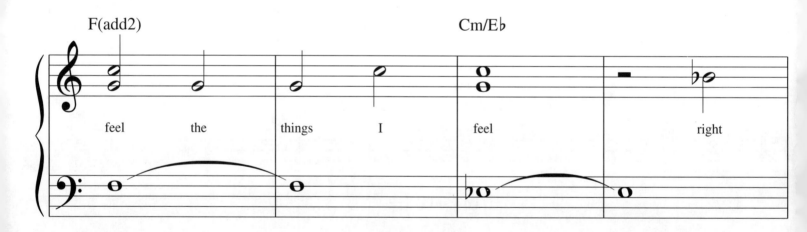

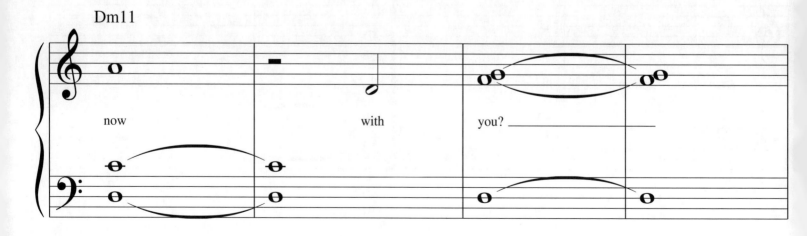

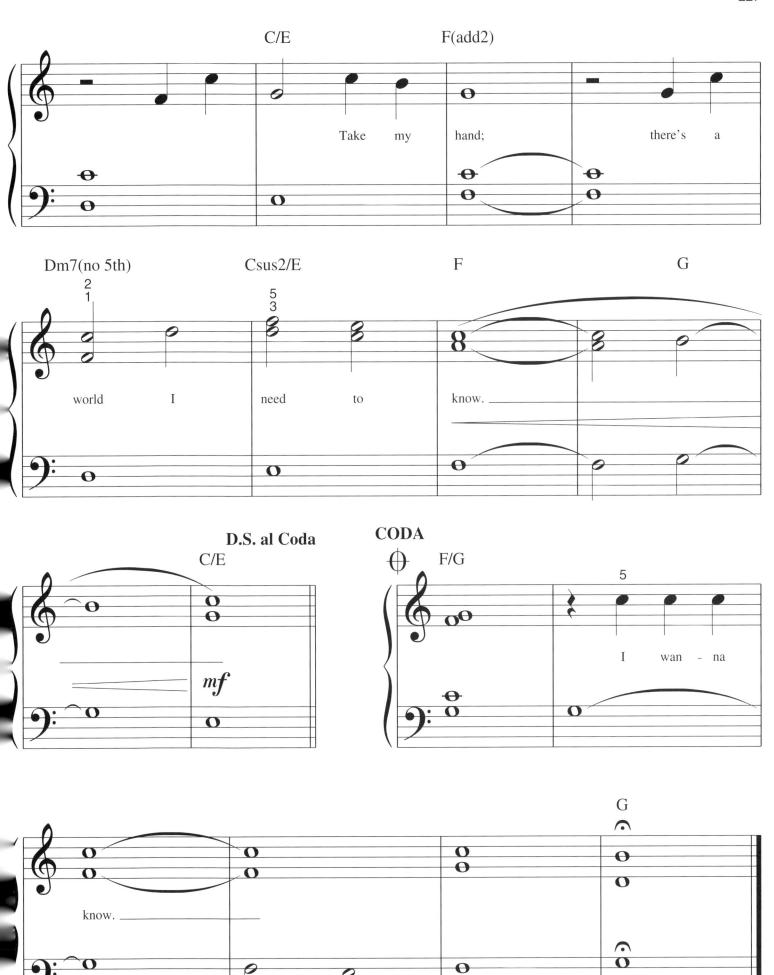

TWO WORLDS

from Walt Disney Pictures' TARZAN™

Words and Music by
PHIL COLLINS

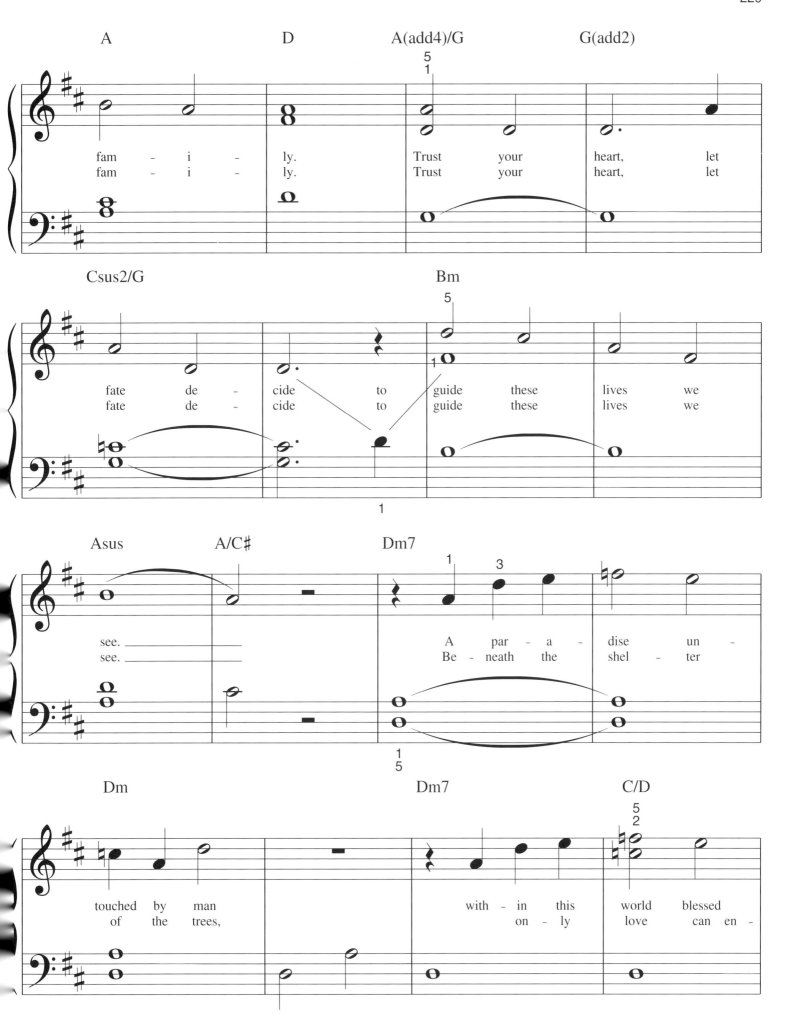

231

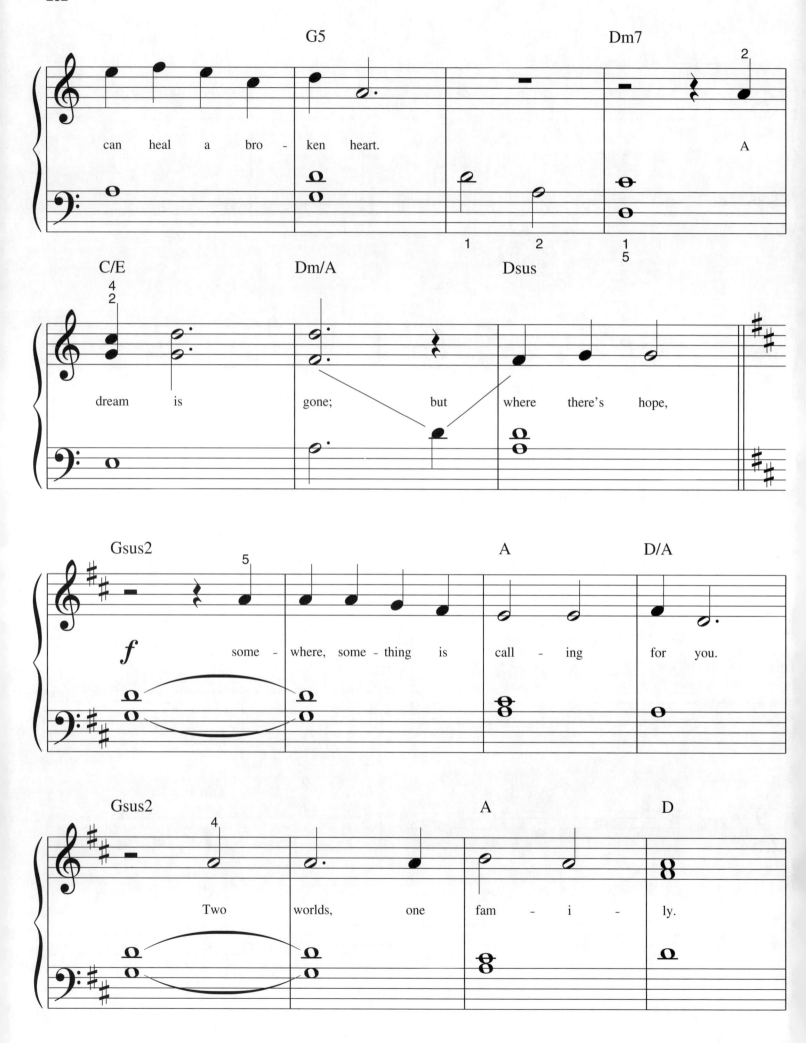

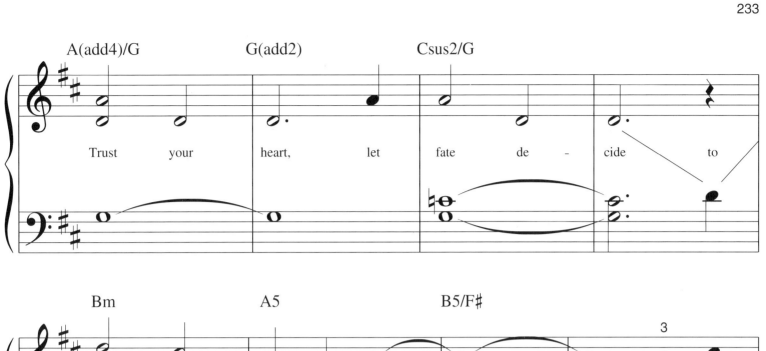

A(add4)/G   G(add2)   Csus2/G

Trust   your   heart,   let   fate   de - cide   to

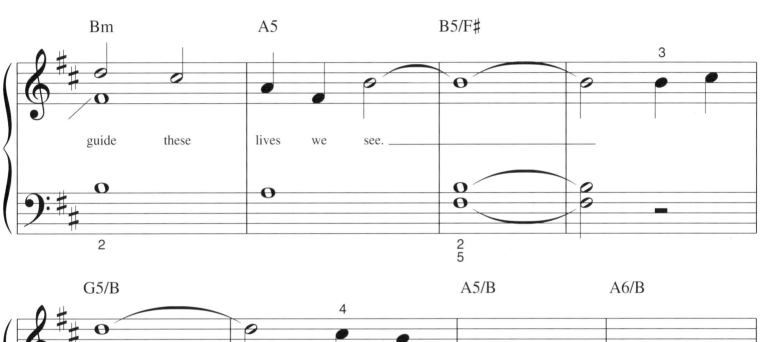

Bm   A5   B5/F#

guide   these   lives   we   see. _____

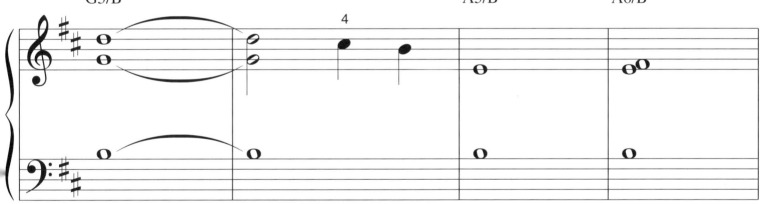

G5/B   A5/B   A6/B

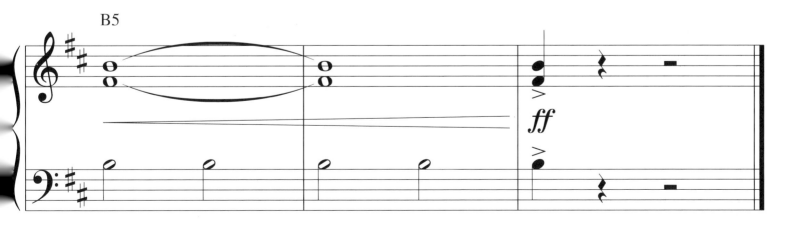

B5

ff

YOU'LL BE IN MY HEART
(Pop Version)
from Walt Disney Pictures' TARZAN™

Words and Music by
PHIL COLLINS

Moderately, in "2"

mp Come stop your cry - ing; ___ it will be all right.

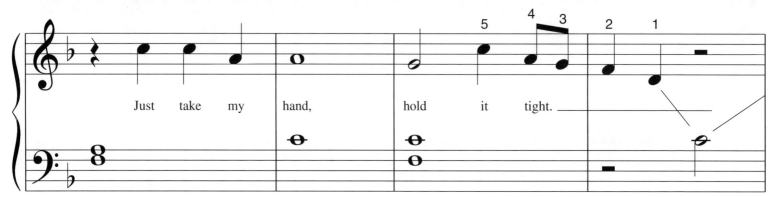

Just take my hand, hold it tight.

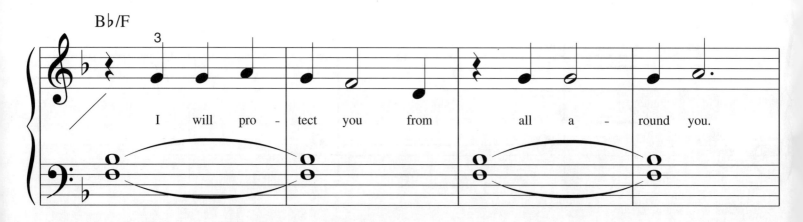

I will pro - tect you from all a - round you.

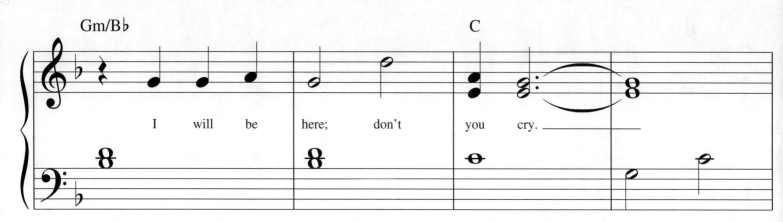

I will be here; don't you cry. ___

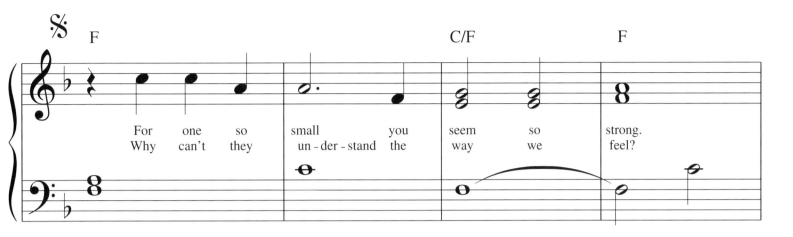

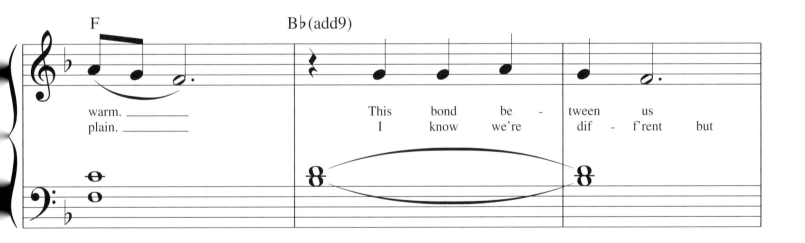

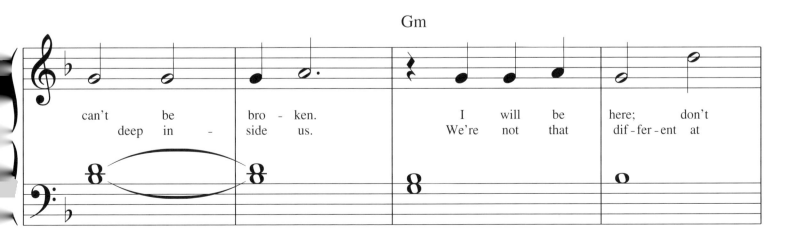

238

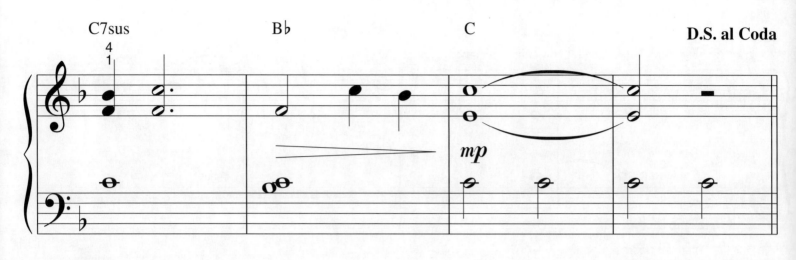

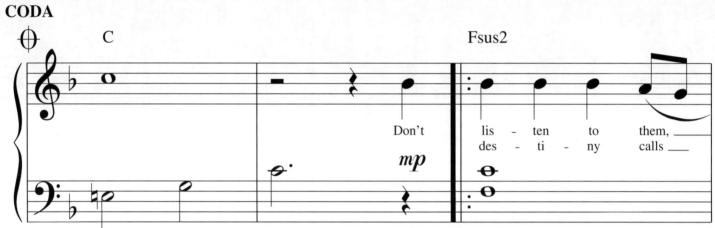

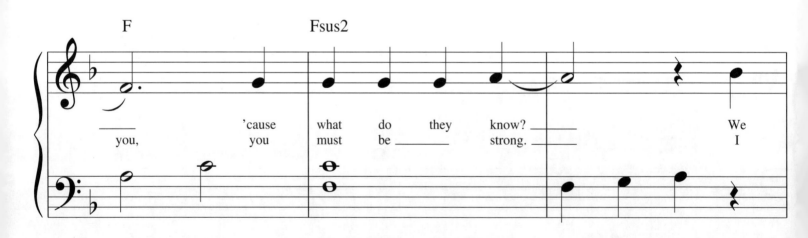

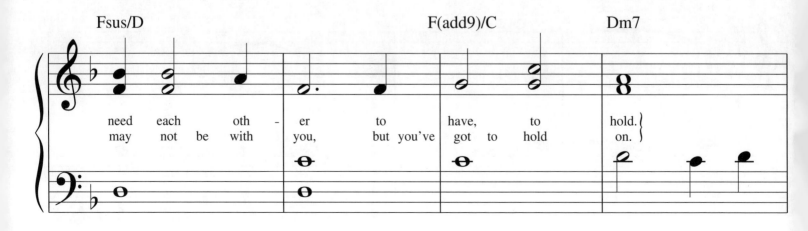

241

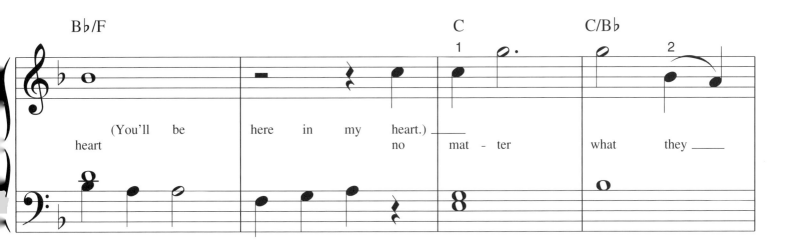

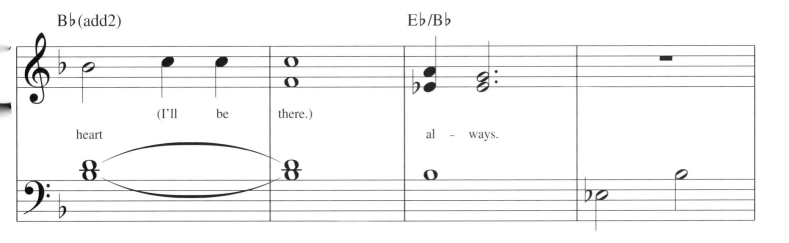

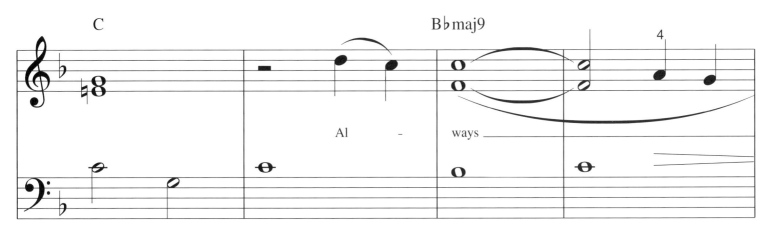

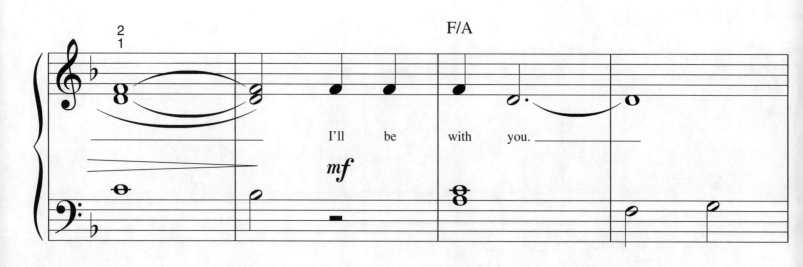

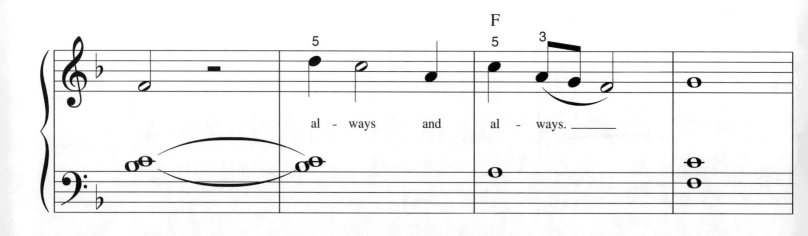

YOU'VE GOT A FRIEND IN ME

from Walt Disney's TOY STORY

Music and Lyrics by
RANDY NEWMAN

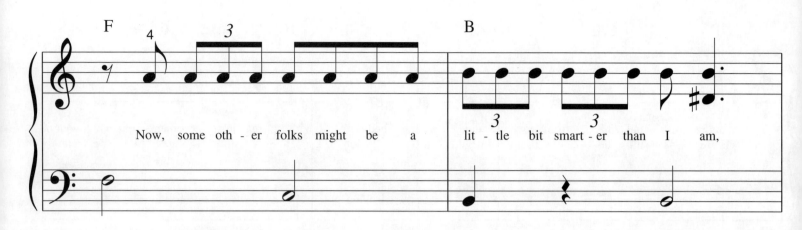

Now, some oth - er folks might be a lit - tle bit smart - er than I am,

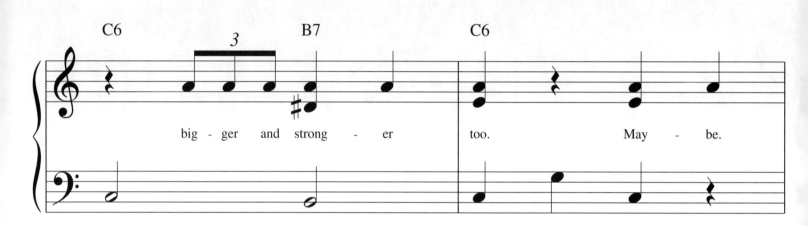

big - ger and strong - er too. May - be.

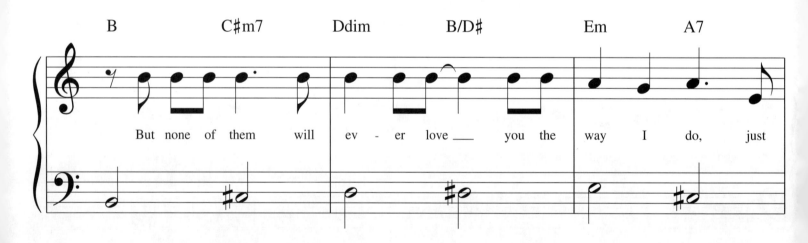

But none of them will ev - er love ___ you the way I do, just

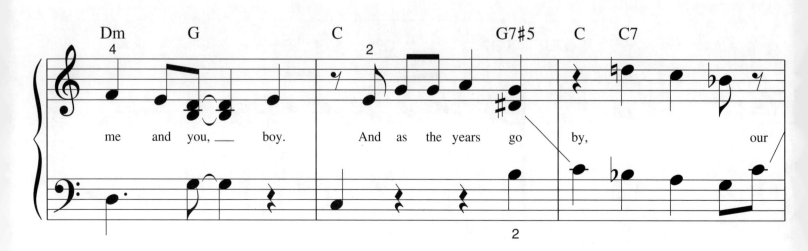

me and you, ___ boy. And as the years go by, our

WHEN SHE LOVED ME

from Walt Disney Pictures' TOY STORY 2 - A Pixar Film

Music and Lyrics by
RANDY NEWMAN

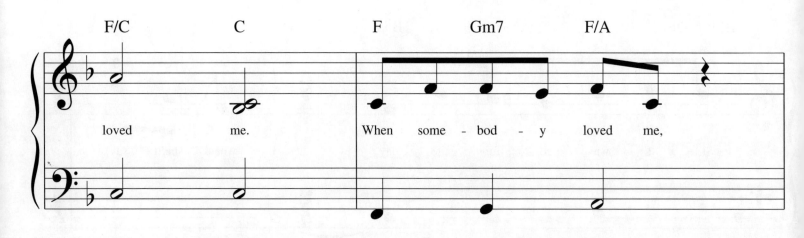

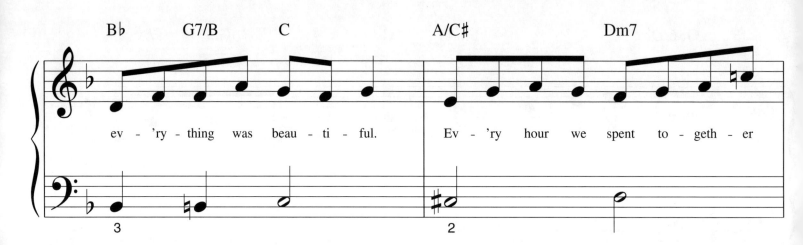

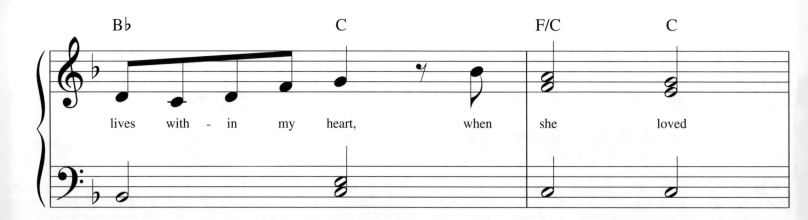